Special People

THE PSYCHOLOGY IN ACTION SERIES

ROBERT LIEBERT, *General Editor*
SUNY State University, Stony Brook

Within the last twenty years, psychologists have begun to apply the sophisticated tools of psychological research to problems that directly affect our daily lives—personal fulfillment, better relationships, child development, and other such issues.

In the PSYCHOLOGY IN ACTION series, the authors apply the results of this research to problems encountered in everyday life, making today's psychological advances accessible to students, parents, teachers, and the general reader.

SHIRLEY COHEN is Assistant Professor of Education, Hunter College and Director of the Special Education Development Center, The Center for Advanced Study in Education, Graduate School and University Center of the City University of New York. In this capacity she has produced a variety of training materials for teachers and parents, as well as *Accepting Individual Differences,* a curriculum for children that is designed to foster increased acceptance of the disabled.

Special People

A Brighter Future for Everyone with Physical, Mental, and Emotional Disabilities

SHIRLEY COHEN

A SPECTRUM BOOK

Prentice-Hall, Inc., *Englewood Cliffs, New Jersey 07632*

Library of Congress Cataloging in Publication Data

Cohen, Shirley
  Special people.

  (The Psychology in action series) (A Spectrum Book)
  Includes bibliographies and index.
  1. Handicapped. 2. Handicapped children. I. Title.
II. Series. [DNLM: 1. Handicapped. 2. Rehabilita-
tion. HD7255 C678s]
HV3000.C63   362.7'8'4   77-2153
ISBN 0-13-826511-9
ISBN 0-13-826503-8 pbk.

HV
3000
C63

Quotation by Betty Pieper is from D. Biklen, *Let Our Children Go: An
Organizing Manual for Parents and Advocates*. Syracuse: Human Policy Press,
1974, pp. 43–44. Reprinted by permission.

© 1977 by PRENTICE-HALL, INC., ENGLEWOOD CLIFFS, NEW JERSEY 07632

A SPECTRUM BOOK

Printed in the United States of America

1   2   3   4   5   6   7   8   9   10

Prentice-Hall International, Inc., *London*
Prentice-Hall of Australia Pty. Limited, *Sydney*
Prentice-Hall of Canada, Ltd., *Toronto*
Prentice-Hall of India Private Limited, *New Delhi*
Prentice-Hall of Japan, Inc., *Tokyo*
Prentice-Hall of Southeast Asia Pte. Ltd., *Singapore*
Whitehall Books Limited, *Wellington, New Zealand*

During the long, hot summers, he sits alone in his wheelchair watching shadows, leaves, and TV game shows. . . . In the beginning of the summer, when Julie's friends come in groups, excitedly savoring their freedom, and she leaves with them, Jeff chokes up and his eyes redden with the strain of holding back tears. Sometimes he bursts out crying, but softly, when I ask what is wrong.

BETTY PIEPER

To Joy
and
to the children with disabilities who were my teachers
and
to their parents

Contents

Introduction

Kim is 5 years old. She has blue eyes and blond curls. She is interested in everything. She laughs. She names the letters of the alphabet. She notices a crack in the linoleum and wonders how it got there. Then Kim slumps over in her chair, her head and torso hanging. She sits there that way until her teacher straightens her up again. Kim cannot move her body. She has cerebral palsy.

What will the future hold for Kim? The exact path and destination can't be plotted, but it will be a better future than she would have had at any time before. It will be better because people are working for Kim, working with her. They haven't given up her body; they haven't given up on her mind or spirit. Kim hasn't given up either. She struggles to make her hands grasp a wooden letter and struggles some more to drop the letter into its place on a form board. "I knew I could do it," she says.

Of the 83.8 million children up to the age of 21 in the United States in 1970 more than 9 million were handicapped (Kalalik et al., 1973, p. 1). Approximately 25,000 babies with cerebral palsy are born each year. Many of these children are not as lucky as Kim. Their minds as well as their bodies have been hurt. Some can't talk clearly enough to be understood; their mouths and faces are distorted by the effort. Many have visual problems or hearing impairments or both.

The brain of a cerebral-palsied person is damaged. It can't control the body's muscles. The person with cerebral palsy may have to learn through intensive practice to do all of what to us are little things, things we do automatically like turning our heads to look at someone who speaks to us, or bringing a cup to our mouths. Even if he masters these, an equally formidable task faces the person with cerebral palsy. He has to learn how to live with the fear, the revulsion, the turning away of many of his fellow human beings. We have come a long way in understanding and living with the handicapped, but we still have far to go in humanizing ourselves and our society so that the handicapped will not be hurt more.

According to the dictionary, a handicap is some form of contest in which difficulties are placed upon superior competitors or advantages given to inferior ones so as to equalize their chances of winning. What a marvelous, truly democratic concept! What a pity that we apply it only to games. There is another meaning of the word "handicapped." It refers to something that hampers a person's functioning and places him at a disadvantage. At least 10 percent of our population may be thought of as handicapped. It is in the everyday lives of these people that the concept of giving advantages to disadvantaged contestants is desperately needed. The contest is living. The goal is a decent life. Unfortunately, there are often no advantages given to these disadvantaged competitors, or the advantages provided are more than offset by the special burdens that are placed upon them.

Burdens can take many forms. When a deformed person is shunned, he bears a special burden. When a paraplegic cannot afford to purchase a car with hand brakes, he bears a special burden. When a deaf child must leave his family in order to obtain an education, he bears a special burden. When a person in a wheelchair is deprived of access to our great museums, he bears a special burden. When an emotionally disturbed child is excluded from school, he and his family bear a special burden. Many people who are handicapped today have impairments that could not have been prevented, given the level of our understanding of genetics and medicine. But many of these same people could be living more productive lives if we cared, if we were just, if we were democratic.

FEAR

Perhaps the major reason why the handicapped suffer is that we are afraid of them. They are different. Different from what we have come to expect. Different from what we value and idealize. Different from what we consider normal. What we perceive as different, as normal, or as valuable depends upon the experiences we have had. The young child builds up a set of expectancies about people—how they look and how they act. The broader the experience base the child has, the broader will his range of expectancies be. The child who has never seen a person wearing eyeglasses will perceive such a person as different. The same will hold true when the child has never seen someone wearing braces or using a wheelchair. However, a child who has grown up in an environment in which people with eyeglasses, hearing aids, canes, braces, or wheelchairs are common will not perceive these individuals as abnormally different.

We don't always fear people whom we perceive as different, or consider them abnormal. When we perceive a person as having more than usual of something that we value, we are in awe of him. We are in awe of the genius. We perceive him as having more intelligence or creativity than we do. We are in awe of extremely beautiful people. We are in awe of extremely talented people. They all have more of something we would like to have. This is not the case when the person is handicapped. We perceive the handicapped person as being different in the sense of having less of something. He is missing something that we have and value.

When a young child comes upon an obviously handicapped individual, someone who is different from those he has known, he does not necessarily show signs of fear or rejection. Some children do. These are often children who cling to the known, who are afraid to move out to explore the environment, whose major strivings are for security and safety. Other children are curious explorers intent upon learning about everything they can. They might initially react to an obviously handicapped individual with wariness, but their drive to understand would soon overcome this. Then they might ask questions and watch carefully and ask more questions until they were satisfied that they understood what they could about the handicapped person, and about themselves in relation to this person.

I once took a child in a wheelchair to a playground. He had cerebral palsy. He couldn't talk. He drooled. He grimaced as if in pain because he could not control his facial muscles. His arms moved in erratic patterns. But he could enjoy the water sprinkler on a hot day. A few of the mothers in the playground immediately took their children and left. Some children moved away to other parts of the playground. Two little girls watched David from a distance. Slowly they inched their way toward him. One looked about 4½, the other was about a year younger. The bigger one finally asked, "Why is he in that chair?" Then, "Can he talk?" "Does he like the water?" "Should I give him some water?" The smaller girl watched everything but said nothing. The older girl played with David for about twenty minutes, pouring water from her bucket onto his hands, until it was time for us to leave.

Having grown up without exposure to individuals with serious deformities, many of us experience an initial shock upon meeting such a person. The initial shock may be something we cannot control, but the behavior that follows is another matter. And it may well be possible to prevent even this initial shock, once the handicapped are accepted into our communities and our homes.

The handicapped sometimes violate our expectations in that their behavior does not follow predictable patterns. Expectations about how people behave probably begin in the first year of life. In a monograph on the reactions of infants to unfamiliar persons, Bronson (1972) offers the hypothesis that the basis for "stranger anxiety"—a reaction of distress which infants begin to exhibit at about 6 months of age—may be the unpredictability of the behavior of the unfamiliar adult. By the time children reach school age they expect that certain kinds of behavior will follow other kinds of behavior, that certain kinds of behavior will be exhibited in some situations but not in others, by some kinds of people but not by others. Seriously disturbed, mentally retarded, and "brain-injured" people often violate out behavioral expectations. Because we cannot predict their behavior we cannot control it, and this often makes us fearful of such people. As a child I was terrified of the special class for retarded children in my school. One day as I had passed this class in a corridor a boy hit out at me for no reason that I could fathom. I had not intentionally done anything to hurt him; I had not accidentally hurt him. I didn't even know him. His behavior didn't make sense to me. It was not something I could not have anticipated and taken steps to avoid. It was not this one tiny wisp of a boy who frightened me. It was the unpredictable quality of his behavior that frightened me. I shunned all the children in this class thereafter.

There is another reason why we are afraid of the handicapped. We are afraid of "catching handicap germs." My daughter taught me this when she was 5. She had been brought together with a 6-year-old multiply handicapped girl for some videotaping. This child was one of the approximately 9,000 deaf-blind children produced by the rubella epidemic in 1964. She was also crippled. She didn't speak but produced screeching sounds. She smelled everything around her. She grasped and then mouthed everything she could. She was trying to learn about and act upon her environment in the only ways she knew. My daughter watched her, but at some distance. At my suggestion she offered part of her snack to Mari. Mari tasted one of the cheese twists and then spit it out. She had never tasted this before and wasn't having any of it. My daughter didn't say a word in the hour or so that she and Mari were together, highly unnatural behavior for my loquacious child. When we were on our way home I asked my daughter why she hadn't spoken and why she had stayed so far away from Mari. "I was afraid of catching handicap germs," she said.

It is not only children who are afraid of catching handicap germs. A superstition common among Jews of Eastern European descent is that a pregnant woman may harm her unborn child if she looks at a deformed person. Most adults are not this literal. We know that we can't catch "handicap germs," that there is no such thing. We know it with our minds, but when faced with a handicapped individual, many of us act as if we don't accept what our minds tell us. We shun close contact. An observer might easily conclude from our avoidance behavior that we are afraid of "catching" something bad, and in a sense we are.

The fear of becoming handicapped is strong, and handicapped people arouse in us an awareness of our own vulnerability, an awareness that we would rather push from consciousness. There is a children's book, *About Handicaps* (Stein, 1974), written by a woman with marvelous psychological insight. She tells the story of a little boy who is frightened of another child's crooked legs and funny walk. He becomes worried about the intactness of his own body and his control over it. He begins to feel that something is very wrong with his own little toes. Some of us feel sick in the presence of handicapped people because the thought that we could become blind or crippled or lose a limb is more than we can handle; even the thought that we might have been born with a disability (but weren't) is more than we can deal with, in the face of a person with such an impairment.

Fear can make people do many things. It can make them withdraw from and shun the object of their fear. It can cause rejection, disparagement, and mockery. Some of the best research on how people react to those with handicaps was done by Jerome Siller. In a study of the dimensions of attitudes toward the handicapped, he and his colleagues found two factors common to the three types of disability studied—blindness, amputation, and cosmetic conditions. The two factors were "interaction strain" and "rejection of intimacy" (Siller et al., 1967, p. 24). In the presence of handicapped people we feel uneasy, nervous, uncomfortable. We reject close relationships with handicapped people.

This uneasiness was experienced by David Huffman when he contemplated getting first-hand information about blindness in preparation for acting the role of a blind man in *Butterflies Are Free.*

> When I started the show I knew absolutely nothing about blindness. I had never come in contact with blind persons . . . consequently I grew up with all the false notions and misconceptions about blindness that most people do. Therefore, I was very self-conscious about seeking aid for the preparation of the role. So self-conscious in fact, I wound up not seeking any aid. (Huffman, 1972, pp. 71–72)

LABELS

Still there are a few pieces missing in the puzzle. Why can we not overcome our initial shock at deformities or impairments, and reject the primitive notion of the contagiousness of handicaps? Why do we continue to reject close relationships with the handicapped? One answer lies in the power of words.

Handicap is a matter of degree. All of us are handicapped in some ways. The woman who is unattractive or obese is handicapped in casual social contacts—that is, her looks cause her to be at a disadvantage in such situations. The man who is very short is handicapped—i.e., placed at a disadvantage by his height, in obtaining certain kinds of jobs which entail impressing clients. The person whose IQ is 110 may be handicapped in a Ph.D. program in which most of the other students have IQs over 125. The child who is tone deaf may be handicapped in his music classes. The child who is very active physiologically and physically may be handicapped throughout his school career because school activities are largely sedentary. We recognize the disadvantages such characteristics cause individuals. We may even say, "She is really handicapped by her looks," or, "That child is going to have a real problem in school." Yet we don't think of these individuals as handicapped. We think of them as people with selected characteristics that place them at a disadvantage. But at some point along the continuum of characteristics that cause people to be at a disadvantage we begin to refer to people as handicapped people; not as people with disabilities or impairments. When we think of a person as someone with characteristics that are likely to be of a disadvantage to him, we still perceive him primarily as someone generally similar to ourselves. When we label and begin to think of a person as handicapped, we see him as different and apart from ourselves. His primary identification for us becomes his impairment or disability. His abilities, his similarities with other people, are lost to us, or become something that surprises us when we cannot ignore them.

My daughter, who was almost 6 at the time, attended a national convention of the Council for Exceptional Children with me. The person who chaired one of the panels at which I was making a presentation was blind. So was his wife Judy. Since the program was to last almost four hours, I asked Judy if she could take care of my daughter. They were both to sit in the audience, but I didn't think my daughter would make it through the whole program. After about an hour and a half I noticed them leaving the room and didn't see them again until the program had been completed.

My daughter loved Judy. She wanted to know when she would see her again. She and Judy had had a great time. They had played counting games and finger games. They had bought snacks in a cafeteria. They had sung songs. When I happened to mention something about Judy's blindness, my daughter stopped. "Judy is not blind," she said. "Her husband is, but not Judy." When I again stated that Judy was blind, my daughter recited a long list of all the things that Judy had done with her as proof that this could not be so. My daughter, at age 5, could not conceive of a blind person as being so able.

The labeling of a person as handicapped reflects how we think about this person, but also shapes our future thinking about him. People with disabilities have recognized this power of labels in shaping perception and thought. Organizations of and for the handicapped have pushed for the elimination of certain labels and the substitutions of others. We no longer refer to certain kinds of children as Mongoloids. We say that they have Down's Syndrome, the medical term for their condition. We no longer use terms like idiot and imbecile for the mentally retarded. We speak of moderately retarded, severely retarded, and profoundly retarded. We no longer call people crippled. We say that they have physical handicaps or orthopedic handicaps. The term "handicapped" is itself currently in disrepute in some quarters. What is being pushed as a substitute is the term "disabled." The thinking behind this move is that "handicapped" connotes inability to function adequately, a condition which the disabled consider more a result of the way society responds to them than a result of their impairments per se. A paraplegic is a disabled person, but he is handicapped only when society blocks his access, both literally and figuratively, to the world of school or work or socialization. If he cannot work, not because he lacks the skills demanded by the job, but because the absence of ramps makes it impossible for him to enter the building in a wheelchair, then he is handicapped.

Unfortunately this change of label in itself is not likely to effect the change of thinking which people with impairments would like to see. Nor is the even more appropriate but cumbersome multi-word label, "person with a disability." Much more than a change of label is needed to accomplish this goal.

Before leaving the topic of labels, let's address another basic question: Why not eliminate labeling altogether? In 1972 the United States Secretary of Health, Education and Welfare directed that a major study of the classification and labeling of children, and its consequences, be conducted. Nine agencies within HEW sponsored and participated in this work. After two years the final report was ready. The primary conclusion of the study was:

> We do not concur with sentiments, widely expressed, that classification of exceptional children should be done away with. Although we understand that some people advocate the elimination of classification in order to get rid of its harmful effects, their proposed solution oversimplifies the problem. Classification and labeling are essential to human communication and problem solving; without categories and concept designators, all complex communicating and thinking stop . . . we do not wish to encourage the belief that abuses can be remedied by not classifying. (Hobbs, 1975, p. 5)

DISTORTED IMAGES

All but the most severely and multiply impaired individuals have abilities as well as disabilities. People with disabilities are more than the sum of their impairments. They want to be perceived in terms of their strengths as well as their weaknesses, their similarities as well as their deviations or differences. They want to be seen as individuals.

> Perhaps the most common plaint in the literature by blind persons is that they are rarely accepted and judged as individuals who may have a particular assortment of capacities and deficiencies. . . . Their blindness, according to reports by blind persons appears to overwhelm all other attributes they possess, and dominates the responses they receive from sighted persons they may encounter. The fact of blindness penetrates into every aspect of the relationships in which they engage. This cannot be accounted for simply by the deficiency in vision. (Lukoff, 1972, p. 1)

We expect the disabled to be either very nice or very bad or very bitter, a kind of Captain Hook or Little Lame Prince. Some do, in fact, fit these expectations, but only in part because they are disabled. It is true that some people with disabilities depend upon assistance from others in many settings, and, therefore, need to act in such a way as to assure the offer of this assistance. It is also true that some people are bitter about being disabled or about the obstacles which society puts in their paths because of their impairments. But people with disabilities exhibit the full range of personality and character variations possible to human beings. Some are leaders, some followers; some are basically competent, others incompetent; some are friendly, others unfriendly; some are angry, some are content and fulfilled. Most of the disabled are a combination of all these characteristics, just as you and I are. The presence or absence of a characteristic that is labeled a disability is very seldom the sole or even primary reason for these variations in personality. Variations among people with disabilities arise from the same factors that give birth to them in anyone, particularly family relationships and childrearing approaches. People with disabilities are neither better nor worse people than we are. They are people like us.

I recently read a book called *If You Could See What I Hear*, which was written by a blind man and a collaborator (Sullivan and Gill, 1975). Several things about this autobiography bothered me. After analyzing this feeling of dissatisfaction I realized that one aspect of the book that disturbed me was its frequent reference to the sexual activities of this blind man. The same kind of reports in an autobiography of a man who was not disabled would not have bothered me, but somehow because this man was blind his lust annoyed me. I wanted him to be better, more moral, purer, because he had a disability. It's almost as if he were spoiling a cause. Why couldn't he be like Margaret Lester, the subject of another biography of a disabled person (Epstein, 1969). Margaret Lester, although paralyzed from the chest down, somehow became pregnant, gave birth to, and raised three children. She was the perfect wife, mother, and example for other paraplegics. She was cheerful and optimistic, worked to exhaustion, and was willing to try anything to expand her independence. She was a shining model. Tom Sullivan was bright, talented, and ambitious, but he was also egocentric and self-indulgent. He was neither angel nor black sheep, but somewhere in the grey in-between. We are not used to thinking about disabled people as being in this middle ground with most of the rest of us.

IGNORANCE

We feel uncomfortable with persons who are disabled because we don't know how to act with them. We are afraid of saying the wrong thing, of not doing something we should, of doing something we shouldn't. When we happen to mention something about "seeing" in the presence of a blind person we feel uneasy, as if we had said a taboo word, as if blind people don't know that others can see. When a deaf person is present we almost shout our conversational communications. When we are with a person who has a problem with motor control, such as most cerebral-palsied persons do, we may hover about him constantly trying to relieve him of all movement tasks or we may shrink from offering help altogether. We don't know what is appropriate, and we are afraid to ask. Out own ambivalent feelings toward the disabled make us afraid to ask.

A very simple way to make people feel less uncomfortable with the disabled is to teach them how to behave in the presence of a person with an impairment. This would save disabled people a lot of grief too! A woman who became blind in later life wrote a wonderfully funny but important little book called *See It My Way* (Swieringa, 1973). In this book, which she wrote to help her family and friends adjust to her as a person without vision, the author tells of all kinds of calamities caused by well-meaning people who wanted to help.

> One evening some dear friends told me to leave my cane in the car. They wanted me to feel at ease with them. As they started to walk — one on either side of me — each took me by an arm. In this three-abreast fashion, we tried to go into a building. But I stumbled on the threshold and bop! I hit my head on the door casing. (no pagination)

What her friends should have done was the following:

> One person should assume the role of guide. Let me carry my cane in one hand as I hold onto your arm with the other hand. I need the security of being able to probe ahead with my cane to detect unusual objects.

And instead of shunning references to visual images when you are with a blind person, share them. "Let me see things with you," says Marilyn Swieringa. "A blind person's life can be so much more interesting if you take time to explain what is happening around her."

In our ignorance we dehumanize the disabled. Blind adults whose impairment is not always immediately apparent report that waitresses stop talking to them as soon as their visual impairment is noted. It is as if their blindness has also suddenly made them deaf and mindless.

> So a lot of times I'll go in [to a restaurant], especially with another person, we will sit down and the waitress will come up and say,

"What does *he* want?" And I'll say, "I'd like a hamburger." And then she'll look over at the guy with me again and say, "What does *he* want to drink?" And I'll say, "I'll take a coke." And she'll look back over at the other guy and say, "Does he want any dessert?" I just can't believe it, but that happens pretty often. I don't think it's any real cruelty on the part of the waitress. I don't think she knows how to approach it at all. ("Person to Person," 1973, p. 9)

This "spread-of-defect distortion" is one of the ways by which we dehumanize the disabled.

THE STRUGGLE FOR SELF-ESTEEM

Not only is the way we react toward the disabled important in itself, but it is also important because it affects the way people with disabilities think of themselves. To a large extent the way we see ourselves is a reflection of the way others appraise us. If these appraisals are consistently or consensually negative, they cannot help but influence the child's conception of himself and what he is willing to try. In his autobiography Raymond Goldman describes the shame and inferiority he felt upon learning, at age 8, how his peers perceived his paralyzed and withered legs.

One of the boys leaned down and touched my leg. He circled it with thumb and forefinger. "Look how skinny!" he shouted trium-phantly. "I can wrap it with two fingers!"

"Let's see!"

"Sure 'nough!"

"Gee, what skinny old legs!"

A feeling of inferiority began to batter against the bulwark of my illusions. I sensed the ridicule before I comprehended it.

. . . A few ill-mannered boys had implanted in me the seed of shame from which I was to conceive a monster. (Wright, 1960, p. 146)

Reactions other than rejection may also hurt. Pity may shake a child's developing concept of himself as someone who is able, who can become a competent doer. Sometimes this pity takes the form of expressions of compassion or commiseration for the mother, often in the presence of the child even when the child is capable of understanding this communication. The "disabled-as-an-it syndrome" shows itself again in these communications. The disabled child who is subjected to such communications must fight against beginning to perceive himself in this way — as an "it" and as a burden.

Many of the disabled and their families are now in conflict over telethons and other fundraising activities that feature children with impairments. One of the reasons for this conflict is the belief that such activities are designed to arouse pity, and perhaps guilt, feelings that may well interfere with the conception of disabled individuals as competent, and that may result in increased strain in face-to-face interactions. People with disabilities, and parents of the disabled, are trying to erase the image of the disabled as beggars in need of mercy. Such an image is incongruent with what the disabled want to achieve and are achieving increasingly today.

> When will we all face the truth that the telethons, poster children, and on, and on, exploit our children? The exposure of the telethon is the closest that many people will ever come to a child with a handicapping condition. Sure, as they watch, tears come to their eyes — before they call in their donations. But the tears are . . . for that poor, pitiful crippled kid who can barely hold his balance to walk across the stage. . . .
>
> We all work so hard to understate our children's disabilities, and to stress his abilities. Then we very foolishly and mindlessly allow it to be sold down the tube by perpetuating the helpless invalid image which society has of our children. ("Point/Counterpoint," 1975, p. 40)

This drive to change the image of the disabled as helpless creatures in need of mercy is exemplified by the work of one mother of a multiply handicapped child. Betty Pieper collected photographs and cartoon drawings of the disabled which highlight their competence, and assembled them to form *The Able Disabled Kit* (Pieper, 1975). She uses this kit in making presentations at meetings throughout New York State and sells it to others for similar purposes. The kit pictures range from cartoons like that of a person in a wheelchair skydiving and saying, "And they said it couldn't be done," to that of a "march" by members of Disabled in Action designed to raise the consciousness of legislators about discrimination against disabled people.

Sometimes parents and teachers of children with disabilities are perceived as cruel by people who observe their interactions with their disabled children or pupils.

> I'll never forget the time I was in a big shopping center parking lot with my mother one day. We had gone out shopping. And it was still while I was learning how to put it [the wheelchair] in [a car]. And I said, "You just stand there and I'll try to put it in myself. And if it falls, at least you will be there, but it will be a good practice session."
>
> So she said, "O.K." And I'm really struggling and I see some man all the way at the other end of the parking lot—and he's coming, I see him walking toward us. I'm struggling, I am always the most awkward person in the world doing this. And I'm struggling putting this thing in the car and this man comes up, "Hey lady (talking to my mother), who the hell do you think you are? Why don't you help her? You think you're so goddamned smart just standing there." ("Person to Person," Part III, 1973, pp. 47–48)

What appeared as cruelty to this casual observer was the determination of a physically disabled young person to achieve maximum independence and the strength of her mother in supporting this determination.

Pity was perhaps a reaction that was helpful to the disabled in the past when their survival depended upon the charity that came from it, and when the alternative to pity was rejection. The alternatives are no longer limited to pity or rejection. While there is still a place for compassion, the drive today is for the development of maximum competence, the recognition of rights, the provision of opportunities, and the willingness to relate to the disabled as individual human beings.

Don't Feel Sorry for Paul (Wolf, 1974) is the name of a remarkable children's book, remarkable both for its messages and because it has been published. Just five years ago it could not have happened. Paul is a boy of 7 who is deformed. On one hand he has no fingers, on one foot no toes. On his good hand he had only an enlarged thumb and a webbing-together of two fingers, on his good foot only a big toe. He wears three prosthetic devices to substitute for his missing body parts. Through photographs and words we learn about Paul's life. We see him putting on his prostheses in the morning and taking them off in the evening so that he can wrestle with his father. We see him getting training in how to use his hook to cut with a knife and in learning how to ride a horse. We see him playing, doing, loving, and being loved. The message is, Paul will make it. He is able. He has nothing to hide, or be ashamed of. Paul's mother concludes (p. 20), "Don't feel sorry for Paul. He doesn't need it."

The disabled have confounded their professional discouragers. Children with Down's Syndrome have learned to read and write. Amputees have learned to ski. Paraplegics have learned to live independently. The blind have become teachers of sighted children. In the preface of an autobiography written by his son who has Down's Syndrome, a father writes:

> About a fortnight after Nigel's birth, his mother and I were told that no matter how much trouble we went to, and no matter how much love and care we gave Nigel, he would be an idiot and that nothing we could do would alter the fact. If we had accepted this, it would have become true. (Hunt, 1967, p. 22)

The disabled and their families are fighting now, fighting for the right to a better life. A great movement has started.

Organizations have been formed, test cases made in the courts, and new laws passed. The disabled are running their own schools and publishing their own magazines. They are supporting bold research that may eventually help the blind to see and the paralyzed to walk. They are negotiating with government and business. Still, the barriers are there. They fall slowly and at great cost.

REFERENCES

BRONSON, G. W., "Infants' Reactions to Unfamiliar Persons and Novel Objects," *Monographs of the Society for Research in Child Development,* 37 (1972), (3, Serial No. 148).

EPSTEIN, J., *Mermaid on Wheels: The Remarkable Story of Margaret Lester.* New York: Taplinger, 1969. Copyright © 1967 by Irene Epstein.

HOBBS, N., *The Futures of Children.* San Francisco: Jossey-Bass, 1975.

HUFFMAN, D., "On Playing Don Baker in *Butterflies Are Free, "* in *Attitudes Toward Blind Persons,* ed. I. F. Lukoff, O. Cohen et al., pp. 71-74. New York: American Foundation for the Blind, 1972.

HUNT, N., *The World of Nigel Hunt: The Diary of a Mongoloid Youth.* New York: Garrett, 1967.

KALALIK, J. S. et al., *Services for Handicapped Youth: A Program Overview.* Santa Monica, Cal.: Rand Corporation, 1973.

LUKOFF, I. F., "Attitudes Toward the Blind," in *Attitudes Toward Blind Persons,* ed. I. F. Lukoff, O. Cohen et al., pp. 1-15. New York: American Foundation for the Blind, 1972.

"Person-to-Person," *The Exceptional Parent,* 3, no. 2 (1973), 7-12.

"Person-to-Person," part III, *The Exceptional Parent,* 3, no. 4 (1973), 45-49.

PIEPER, B., "Some Curricular Experiences for Children," in *Fostering Positive Attitudes toward the Handicapped,* ed. S. Cohen, pp. 111-26. New York: City University of New York, Special Education Development Center, 1975.

"Point/Counterpoint," *The Exceptional Parent,* 5, no. 3 (1975), 39-40.

SILLER, J. et al., *Studies in Reaction to Disability,* XII. New York: New York University, School of Education, 1967.

STEIN, S. B., *About Handicaps: An Open Family Book for Parents and Children Together.* New York: Walker, 1974.

SULLIVAN, T., and D. GILL, *If You Could See What I Hear.* New York: Harper & Row, 1975.

SWIERINGA, M., *See It My Way.* Grand Rapids, Mich.: Institute for the Development of Creative Child Care, 1973.

WOLF, B., *Don't Feel Sorry for Paul.* Philadelphia: Lippincott, 1974.

WRIGHT, B., *Physical Disability: A Psychological Approach.* New York: Harper & Row, 1960.

TWO

On Being the Parent
of a Disabled Child

The birth was quite normal, and Dietlind was conscious of all that
was happening. Suddenly the midwife asked her brutally, "Is your
husband armless by any chance?" "Why?" my wife cried. "You
don't mean that my baby . . ." "Yes. He has only deformed stumps
for arms."*

The worst had happened. That first, almost instinctive question
which mothers of newborns ask: "Is my baby normal?" had been
answered in a terrifying way. Dietlind was only one of hundreds
of new parents whose question was answered this way between
1958 and 1962. These were the parents of what were called
"thalidomide babies." In West Germany alone about 6,000
babies were born deformed during this period because their
mothers had taken a tranquilizer containing the drug
thalidomide during the first trimester of their pregnancies. Two
little white pills had cost Dietlind's baby its two arms.

*From K. H. Schulte-Hillen, "My Search to Find the Drug That Crippled My Baby,"
in W. C. Kvaraceus and E. W. Hayes, *If Your Child Is Handicapped* (Boston: Porter
Sargent, 1969), p. 38.

Not all parents learn that their child is disabled shortly after its birth. Sometimes the baby is a beautiful, perfectly formed child. It is only later that the parents become concerned, when the child's eyes don't follow a moving toy, or when the child doesn't respond to his mother's voice if his head is turned, or when he hasn't learned to sit up at an age when most children are walking.

> One lovely spring afternoon, when Ronnie was about nine months old, I was sitting in the yard enjoying the sunshine, when a woman approached with twin boys in a stroller. She stopped to visit and I learned the boys were both blind, as a result of too much oxygen administered during incubation following their premature birth. I felt a stab at my heart when comparing my healthy, happy, "normal" son with the twin boys. Little did I know that within the coming year I too would be explaining to people that my son was disabled.
>
> Shortly after the encounter with the twins, Ronnie was stirring from his nap. I went to get him so he could watch me prepare dinner. His back was toward me as I walked into the bedroom, and he was looking out the window. Approaching, I called out to him—but he didn't respond. Drawing nearer, I called his name again, this time a bit louder. Still no response. At the end of his crib I was shouting, but still he didn't turn. As I walked around the crib he saw me and held out his arms. Ronnie was deaf! (Rhodes, 1972, p. 10)

Sometimes parents sense, almost without being able to define how, that something is very wrong:

> She was an unusually quiet baby who did not cry. She seemed strangely unresponsive, and I began to have vague worries that Eva's development was not what it should be. . . . I voiced my concern to our pediatrician.
>
> "I wouldn't worry," he answered. . . .
>
> But as the weeks went by, Eva's slow development became a matter of increasing concern. Arthur, my husband, and I tried to

come to grips with our fears. Anxiously we watched for and discussed with each other every small sign of her progress. (Herz, 1969, p. 110)

I was talking recently to the mother of a child with Down's Syndrome as we drove to pick her daughter up from school. Without any special stimulation, she recounted her experience when her child was born. It was a story I had heard over and over again about a doctor who said, "Don't take it home"; not even "Don't take the baby home"—just don't take this thing, this creature, this "it" home. How many mothers, confused and depressed, have heeded that message only to regret it later, sometimes too late? How many of those institution residents with vacant faces and no words could have been people with some kind of life if they had had homes with someone to love them and teach them?

There is no good way to tell a mother that the child her body has given off after nine months of preparation is damaged. The hurt, the terrible fear, the sense of being punished unfairly, the anger is almost always there. Words cannot take these feelings away. They can only give hope, or make the panic worse. In response to a magazine article a parent wrote:

Although it is now 19 years since my child with Down's Syndrome was born, it is still painful for me to recall the coldness, the brutality and the inhumanity of the manner in which my doctor held my daughter by the nape of her neck, like a plucked chicken, and pointed to her typical mongoloid features. He went on to say that, since my child was a mongoloid (a word, by the way, I had never heard of prior to that day), she would not grow nor develop, and that my husband and I should make plans to place her in an institution, because of the sociological problems involved in bringing up a defective daughter. (Pendler, 1975, p. 34)

Physicians, outside the narrow confines of their medical training, are no different from the rest of us. They have the same prejudices and limitations of the spirit. When a disabled child is born, too few physicians are prepared to offer sensitive but honest communication to the parent:

> "Well," I said, "how is the baby?" He said, "she's very oriental looking." "Well my husband's oriental." He replied that she had a very high cheekbone and slanted eyes. "Well, my husband has high cheekbones and a slant to his eye." He kept stumbling, and I was becoming very suspicious. "Well, it's a very pronounced look, an oriental look." Finally, I asked, "Now, what are you trying to tell me? Is something wrong with my baby? Are you trying to tell me something?" "Uh, well, you want me to be specific?" I said, "You're damn right; I want you to be specific, it's my baby. And I want you to tell me what's wrong." ("Who Cares What Happens to Miriam?" 1973, p. 12)

Unfortunately, most mothers who give birth to disabled children are not only faced with the sad fact of their child's impairment but also with one of those two hurtful reactions from their physicians: treatment of the infant as something less than human or avoidance of their responsibility to inform and support the mother, their patient. Too few physicians are knowledgeable enough to offer the supportive guidance parents need at such a time, while recognizing the parents' rights and responsibilities.

There are, in fact, parents who cannot cope with the experience of having a disabled child. There are other parents who can and who feel that their lives have become richer as a result of having had this experience. But a decision on the future of a human being should not be made in haste, under pressure, at a time of weariness and stress. A parent has a right to see her child and examine her own reactions to her offspring. She has a right to know what the alternatives are and what each of them implies.

There is a common pattern or sequence of reactions that many parents go through after learning that their child is impaired. It begins with shock.

> The shock of the birth of a child like this doesn't come all at once. It's worse in some ways than the death of a child because you gradually realize that this child is never going to live in the fullest

sense of the word. It is only after months or years pass that you find out how your family will be affected.

It was difficult for us to absorb the first shock, which is truly physical as well as mental. We were numb, we could scarcely walk about and do our normal day's work, or talk to other people. (Hosey, 1973, pp. 15–16)

Guilt and feelings of inadequacy often follow.

Assailed by guilt, he would protest to mom that he was responsible. Had he not gone on a wild weekend to Florida with his Irish friends the week before I was born? If he had stayed at home, would my mother have carried the child to full term? Was the blindness of his son some sort of providential punishment for his prodigality? (Sullivan and Derek, 1975, p. 9)

Then a rejection of the diagnosis or prognosis, and a desperate search for a cure.

"Don't worry," I was saying to myself, and then to Joyce as I held her hand. "We'll see other doctors. Even Green admits he may be wrong." . . . we resolved never to call Dr. Green again. A month later I took a six weeks leave from the engineering consultant firm where I worked, checked out all our money from the bank, and set out. . . .

At the end of five weeks we had seen psychiatrists and been to hospitals in Baltimore, New York, Chicago, and Philadelphia. The result was always the same: no hope. The expensive tests and consultation fees, plus hotel and travel expenses, had exhausted our savings. I knew I should return to the office. Still I held back. (Robinson, 1969, pp. 98–101)

When the diagnosis is confirmed and no miraculous cure can be found, there often follows a period of withdrawal and isolation.

We dropped all social contacts: the bridge group, the Sunday school class, Saturday nights at the country club, Sunday evenings with relatives. When we received an invitation, it always seemed easier to beg off. We had a ready-made excuse. We had to take care of Eddie. (Robinson, 1969, p. 102)

Then time forges some kind of resolution. It may mean that the disabled child is assimilated into the life of the family. It may mean that the disabled child is removed from the family altogether or is moved out of it part of the time. It may mean that the family dies because the parents cannot agree on a future. It sometimes means that the life of the family and its individual members is strengthened and enriched.

It is never easy to be the parent of a disabled child, but that does not mean it cannot also be a joy. A mother describes her child: "Stephen is 11 years old, profoundly retarded, cerebral-palsied and epileptic. He doesn't walk or talk and he probably never will. He does not understand speech and has few ways to communicate his needs" (Hosey, 1973, p. 14). Yet on the back of Stephen's wheelchair in big letters is written "TO KNOW ME IS TO LOVE ME."

MY CHILD OR NOT

The first decision parents may be faced with after the birth of a disabled child is whether to accept the child as a member of the family. Ten or fifteen years ago most parents were told by the doctor who delivered their impaired baby not to take it home. Mothers were advised not even to look at the baby. Many parents followed this advice and gave their babies up for a lifetime of institutionalization. They did so almost without thinking. In their state of shock, they relied on the voice of authority. Today the picture is more varied. Some parents are still being given this advice. Others are being counseled, even pressured, into keeping their disabled child at home. The pendulum is swinging in a new direction.

While urging parents to resist pressure from professionals to institutionalize their retarded babies, Linde and Kopp (1973) write:

> Those who help children who are handicapped to become more able, believe that these youngsters possess the potential to develop into worthy persons. Only when the parent becomes convinced

that his child does not possess this spark of promise does he give up, and have the youngster placed in an institution. In our modern world, this action represents a significant act of both resignation and surrender. (pp. 7–8)

Think of the pressure inherent in this statement and the guilt it can engender in parents!

In a sense any advice about long-range decisions that is given soon after the birth of a disabled child is bad advice. Parents need time to absorb the impact of their child's condition, and to explore its effect upon them. They need time to talk, to cry, to plan. They need to know that they don't have to make long-term decisions about their child's future immediately.

The motivation behind the dictum to abandon the disabled infant before ever relating to it was at least in part motivated by the belief that the mother and the rest of the family would be spared anguish, heartbreak, and continuous stress if she gave up her baby before becoming emotionally tied to it. Inherent in this dictum is the premise that a disabled child brings a lifetime of stress for his family. In some cases this is so. In former years this was the case much more often, but changes in attitudes, opportunities, treatment, and supports have reduced greatly the pain of having a disabled child in the family.

Something else has changed too. Society has been going through a consciousness-raising experience. The horrors of Willowbrook and other institutions are common knowledge. The benefits of a caring family on the disabled child's development are being highlighted. Today, parents who gave their child up for institutionalization without first trying to keep the child in the family are likely to experience strong guilt. The parents of a newborn girl with Down's Syndrome rejected their obstetrician's advice to give their baby up. They felt they had to give their daughter a chance. Nine years later the mother, watching her child cheerfully waving good-bye to her classmates, said, "What a terrible waste that would have been."

In only a tiny proportion of cases can we predict in early infancy what a child's achievements or limitations will be. We may know that a baby has cerebral palsy, but we do not know that this will mean a life of dependence. We may know that a child is deformed, but we do not know that the achievements of his mind won't compensate for the distortion of his physique, or that medicine and technology won't combine to overcome the frailties of his body. Many parents today feel better about having given their disabled child the most they could, even if placement away from the family was the eventual outcome, and this separation was painful.

Not everyone is equipped to be the parent of a disabled child. Some of us cannot assume this role or responsibility. If we consider the thousands of cases of children born with healthy minds and bodies who are abandoned or abused each year, we would not wonder at this. There is no screening test, no qualifying examination for parenthood. Disturbed, incompetent, and alcoholic persons become parents every day, along with those of us who are overburdened, disorganized, egocentric, and bored with parenthood. Disability appears everywhere, among those least capable of coping with it as well as among those able to cope.

A young woman turned her four-day-old child over to a Catholic hospital. The little girl had been born with no arms or legs. Her mother said only that she didn't know what to do with such a child. How many of us would? How many of us would have the resources to call upon? Even support and services might not have changed this woman's decision.

Sometimes a child's functioning is so impaired, and the care required by the child so complicated and burdensome to the family, that the parents are forced to consider institutionalization. Bonnie was a severely retarded child with serious physical problems whose parents reached this point after four years. At age 4 Bonnie slept little, still had difficulty swallowing food, and could not eliminate without an enema. She was partially blind and exhibited spastic paralysis in all her limbs. Her mental age was below six months. The choice Bonnie's parents saw was between "letting Bonnie go in order that her parents and brothers and sisters could better fulfill their own capacity for living, or keeping Bonnie and devoting their lives to her care, with the attendant sacrifice of normal family life and the right to the pursuit of personal fulfillment" (Heisler, 1972, p. 81).

When the parents of a healthy baby don't want their child there is usually a viable, often superior alternative—namely, adoption. Waiting lists to adopt children become longer each year. Potential parents are scrutinized intensively, and often even those with excellent qualifications are disappointed. Until very recently the only alternative for the disabled child whose family could not make a home for him was an institution. One of the by-products of advances in birth control technology and the resultant decreased birth rate is that some couples are now choosing to adopt disabled children rather than be childless. Other families were drawn to adopt disabled children by the war in Vietnam, which maimed thousands of the young. Unfortunately, the number of families willing to adopt a child known to have a disability is still miniscule in relation to the need.

Karen is the child born without arms or legs whose mother turned her over to a hospital at four days of age. Karen was lucky. She found a family to belong to. The DeBolts are, to ridiculously understate the situation, unusual. They have fifteen children, nine of them adopted, and those adopted include five children with physical disabilities. The DeBolts adopt handicapped children because of "joy of it all. To see little kids who've had all the dignity crushed out of them regain it through love."[1] In speaking of Karen's adoption Mrs. DeBolt says, "Our main reason was we just loved the whole idea of Karen herself" (Thomas, 1974, p. 62). At age 6 Karen could swing her way up a

---

[1] L. Fosburgh, "They Find Children in Need—And Ask Them to Join the Family," *New York Times*, January 22, 1974, p. 34. © 1974 by The New York Times Company. Reprinted by permission.

staircase on her plastic legs with the help of her crutches, something the doctors predicted she would never be able to do. With her hooks she plays baseball and paints. She makes beds and folds laundry. "Bob and I look upon Karen with complete awe," Mrs. DeBolt says. "We ask God all the time to make us worthy of her. We just hope we can live up to what Karen is— and allow her to be all the things she can be" (Ibid., p. 64).

Few of us have the strength of spirit of the DeBolts, but if only a tiny fraction of healthy families took handicapped children into their homes and lives, there would be an alternative to institutionalization for those whose parents cannot cope with having a disabled child. These children now wait in vain. Having been already twice burdened, first by fate and then by parents who couldn't accept them, they face yet a third blow—exclusion from the primary institution of humankind. Tens of thousands of disabled children who are in institutions could have been loving and learning in families. They are a mark of our frailty.

NOT ALONE

Parents of children with disabilities need to feel that they are not alone. Theodora de Soyza, a mother of a child with Down's Syndrome, having experienced the loneliness of the hospital experience when she was surrounded by mothers of healthy babies, resolved to help other mothers who found themselves in this situation. Why not a visiting mother program—one in which women who gave birth to retarded babies could be put in contact with other mothers who had faced the same experience? Hospitals were reluctant; social workers had doubts. But there is now in the Bronx, New York, a modest version of this idea, operated under the aegis of the mother who conceived it, from the day-care center she helped found (called the These Our Treasures Day Care Center). When a woman gives birth to a retarded baby at any one of several hospitals in this borough, the hospital social worker tells her about this program. If the mother is receptive, an appointment is set up for a home visit as soon as she gets back from the hospital. Her visitor will be a woman who is herself the mother of a retarded child, one who has been selected for her ability to give both hope and help.

There is a long tradition of home visiting in relation to handicapped children, but this service was largely performed by nurses who focused on the physical care of the child. In addition, such visits were largely limited to children with physical impairments. A home visitor who is the mother of a disabled child can help parents with their concerns and fears, as well as with day-to-day management problems. She can bring parents into the kind of kinship groupings some of them need for mutual support when their disabled children are young. The idea of parents helping other parents is so simple that one wonders why it was not put into action years ago, and why it is not spreading more quickly. Undoubtedly, the reluctance of professionals to accept parents as their peers in the helping process accounts for some of this slowness.

I spoke to a woman who had been put in touch with the These Our Treasures Center soon after the birth of her child. She waited a month before calling because she was immobilized by the shock of becoming the mother of a child with Down's Syndrome. "When you first come home," she said, "You're lost. You hear a lot of stories, like how your child will never be able to feed itself, how it will always be a burden. Then you panic." "What did the contact with the Center do for you?" I asked. Mrs. R. replied:

> I don't know what I would have done. It would have been terrible. I would have been lost.

> I was relieved. I personally felt much better. It eases your mind and makes you feel that you're not the only one.

> You see what you child will be able to learn.

> You meet people with the same problem. We help each other. There's always someone to talk to.

We need a lot of help. There's a lot of misinformation. My kid brother is in high school. One day he came home and asked if Stephanie would grow a beard and a penis? They had been talking about it in school, in science class when they were studying genetics. Maybe some of the kids didn't get it right but this is what they thought.

Joyce [the home visitor] asks if you need help. She knows how to direct you. You ask her questions about what to do. You talk. You get information. She's the mother of a multiply handicapped child. It's amazing that she can be helping you.

There are many supportive services available to parents of young, disabled children. There are educational programs for infants, toddlers, and preschoolers. There are counseling and group therapy programs for parents. But there are not enough of these programs to go around. They are still largely funded by federal seed money for model programs or by private funds from organizations for the disabled. Most states still do not assume responsibility for disabled children until they are at least 5 years of age. Sometimes families that need these programs most are the ones that are not included. Obtaining these services is still often a matter of knowing where resources are and how to go about getting them. These are skills largely found in middle- and upper-class, well-educated families. The poor are often the last to know. Among families of the poor it is still not unusual for children with serious hearing impairments or mental retardation not to receive any special services until they are of public school age, because their families didn't know what to do or where to turn. In view of the critical importance of early intervention with such children, such a deprivation can be disastrous in terms of the child's potential development.

And there are desperately needed support programs that are available to very few. The care of a disabled child can be physically and psychologically exhausting, but parents may be deprived of the relief of an occasional night out because they cannot find a babysitter to stay with their child. Vacations may be a thing of the past too. While a "normal" child can very often move in with a grandparent or an aunt for a week or so while the parents go off by themselves, this is rarely the case when a child is disabled. What is needed is widespread respite care programs, in which disabled youngsters could stay with competent families or in small group centers for a couple of days or weeks while their own families recoup their energies.

PARENTS AS TEACHERS

Parents are the primary teachers of their children. We don't often think of them in this way. We think of teaching as something that's done in school and that helps a child learn to read, write, and do arithmetic. We take for granted the learning of language, motor skills, and social mores, all of which take place before age 5. While a mother may not sit with her child in a certain room during a set period of time each day, with a conscious objective in mind, she teaches her child constantly. She teaches him when she says, "No. No. You mustn't hit Michael." She teaches him when she shows him how to dip a spoon into his food and bring it to his mouth. She teaches him when she reads him nursery rhymes or names the parts of his body or counts his fingers. The mother of a healthy child doesn't have to work very hard at her teaching. Her child responds readily. He wants to learn, to be competent, to be effective in his world. His body and his mind cooperate in this venture. The mother of a disabled child usually has to work much harder to help her child achieve this goal. Even when the child is involved in a good educational program and regular therapy sessions, the work of the parents with their child at home may make a critical difference in their child's eventual achievements. More and more programs for young children have recognized this, and now require the active participation of at least one parent in reinforcing and supplementing the efforts of professionals. Parents now guide their disabled children in physical therapy exercises, language training, and perceptual development. They participate in behavior modification programs to achieve socially tolerable behavior and self-help skills. Only rarely today are parents of the disabled still told that the job of teaching their child should be left to professionals. The results of that policy were often disappointing, sometimes disastrous.

Barbara Trace's baby daughter was different from her two other children.

> Joan was a restless, driven child involved largely in seemingless aimless, frustrating, destructive activity. She could or would not accept limits . . . scenes of rage occurred steadily through the day. Sometimes they were triggered by a specific situation, but more often they were not based on anything discernible or comprehensible to us. Her crying dominated the scene during the first two years of her life . . . (Kastein and Trace, 1966, p. 29)

When Joan was 3½ a serious deficiency in her ability to comprehend and use language was identified. Even with regular treatment at a speech clinic her progress in understanding the world around her and in adjusting to it was very slow. She did not seem to know who her mother and father were. She did not respond to either approval or disapproval, sympathy or love. She was still often demanding, tense, even frenzied. Mrs. Trace believed that Joan's behavior would change only after she began to make sense of the events and relationships around her. To help her daughter reach this goal, she began to work with Joan every day.

> We established our formal work sessions in the afternoon. They lasted, depending upon her responses, from one half hour to two hours each day in one long period or in several brief ones. Gradually, I increased these learning periods to three or four hours per day. When Joan tired, we rested at our work table, singing, clapping our hands, or playing with a toy. Then we resumed our work. We shortened this schedule only when I felt that we had already achieved the maximum for the day, and Joan

could not go on any longer. Actually, the teaching process began the moment Joan awoke in the morning and continued until she went to sleep. It was a round-the-clock procedure. I used every opportunity that presented itself to teach words, to reinforce them, and to help her to develop language. (Ibid., p. 57)

For over six years Barbara Trace kept up this schedule of teaching. Most disabled children either don't need or can't benefit from such intensive, long-term instruction from their parents. And few parents would have the skill or stamina to carry out such a program. But Barbara Trace's daughter at age 3 was very much like children who often are labeled autistic. The prognosis for such children is poor. Many of them spend most of their lives in mental institutions or institutions for the retarded. What Barbara Trace gave her impaired child was a chance for a full life.

THE FUTURE

The mother of a 5-year-old child with cerebral palsy said:

We're sort of taught, or we read, that we're not supposed to feel sorry for ourselves. The world says you shouldn't; and, sometimes when I am, I say, I don't care, damn it! I'm not supposed to, but I *do* feel sorry for myself! I do! I do! God, I feel resentful that I'm in the position I am! (Heisler, 1972, p. 58)

The Greenbergs had a son who was labeled autistic (Greenberg, 1970). Noah was unlike Joan Trace in some ways. While his motor development was quite slow right from the start, he spoke some words before he was 2. But in the year between age 2 and 3 he seemed to withdraw more and regress. Josh Greenberg and his wife loved Noah and wanted desperately to help him, but their way was different. They were emotional and short-tempered, and Noah stabbed at their marriage. They ran from specialist to specialist, trying all the "cures" from megavitamin therapy to neurological retraining to behavior modification. They found no cure. Noah was being helped, but his future was uncertain.

> So if he can sleep the way everyone else in his family does and can keep developing his good habits, we're on the way. The way to where? I do not know. (Greenberg, 1970, p. 190)

The uncertainty, and the concern for the future of their child, preys on parents' minds. "What will happen to my child when I am gone?" parents ask themselves. "Who will take care of him, if he cannot take care of himself?" There is no good answer to this question yet, particularly for families of limited or modest means. An institution is no home to an individual who has known a real home, while independent living is not possible for many persons with disabilities. Group residences or homes may prove an answer for some, but at present the planning and execution of such programs is disjointed and uneven. Moreover, too many disabled people fall through the program cracks, going unnoticed and unsupervised until some crisis occurs. What we need is a system of lifelong support for families of the disabled, which would include planned provision for disabled individuals when their parents are no longer able to care for them. In place of the fragmented, episodic, crisis-oriented service most agencies now offer, the Project on Classification of Exceptional Children recommends that

> A family should be able to register a handicapped child with an agency that would assume long-term responsibility for assisting the family in caring for the child. Registration should occur as soon as the handicapping condition is identified, and as early as at birth. The agency should define its role as helper to the family, to the child, and to other significant helpers in the child's life. (Hobbs, 1975, p. 226)

JOYS AND SORROWS

I have painfully and slowly come to learn that I cannot act as a buffer between Josh and the world, though there are frequently times when I want more than anything to protect him from the pain of being so obviously different. . . . I ache for him when I think of all the difficulties that lie ahead of him. (Kovacs, 1972, p. 30)

At the second grade door, Michelle asked if I would stay until the bell rang. I could feel the tension. It's hard enough to be "the new girl," without being the new girl who has just two fingers on each hand and those funny braces on her legs.

Small groups of children began to form, most of them trying not to stare at "the new girl." But I overheard two boys saying, "Look at her!" to everyone who walked by. . . . Michelle didn't speak but the look of discomfort on her face told me that she was only pretending not to hear the children's remarks. . . .

Driving home that day I cried thinking how I'd like to bang those boys' heads together. (Ouellet, 1974, p. 22)

In the beginning, the greatest sorrow for parents of a disabled child is knowing what might have been but won't ever be. Later, it is knowing the hurts that lie ahead for their child, hurts from which they cannot shield him.

The joys of parents of disabled children are as varied as those of any parent, probably even more so, because nothing is taken for granted. What most parents take for granted can be a cause for great rejoicing in the lives of parents of multiply or severely disabled children. When Karen willed herself up the staircase in her home for the first time, the DeBolt family rejoiced. When Joan Trace began to be able to use words her mother had not taught her, Barbara Trace rejoiced. When Josh began to learn to read, no words could express his mother's happiness. When Michelle learned to play the marimba, it was as if she had reached the pinnacle of achievement in music. The greatest joy there can be for parents of a disabled child is to see their child master something his or her disability made difficult, and to know that having mastered this, their child will be one step closer to a full life. The mother of a blind child of 5 writes:

> Oh, how that child delights me! My very greatest delight is watching while she hatches a thought in her mind that's all her own and then sets forth to carry it out. (Ulrich, 1972, p. 72)

PARENTS ON THE MOVE

The stereotype of the mother of a disabled child has been a woman who is overburdened, isolated, ashamed. Fortunately, the reality of this stereotype is declining. In metropolitan areas particularly, and in the middle class particularly, we see a new breed of mothers: healthy and resilient women who have taken on the roles of advocate and teacher, not only for their own children but for the children of others as well.

Although some fathers have been active in helping to found organizations for the disabled, they have traditionally left childrearing to their wives. This was often no less true when a child was disabled than when it was not. Today, with the advent of more flexible sex roles, fathers are more often becoming involved in the process of raising a disabled child, a change that is likely to strengthen the family as well as the child. In recognition of this change, and in a desire to support it, some programs for disabled children now have father's groups, where men can talk about their feelings for their disabled children, and where they can learn about what *they* can do to help their children grow.

The Association for Children with Learning Disabilities reflects this new kind of parent, and embodies the new concept of the role of parents. It represents parent power, parent advocacy, parent partnerships with professionals. Founded by parents in 1964, it stimulated the focusing of professional attention on children who were not clearly retarded but who were often considered dunces because of their special learning problems. This organization was largely responsible for passage of the Learning Disabilities Act of 1969, which established federal aid to the states for model programs and research in this area. It sponsors an annual international conference for professionals as well as parents. It serves as a resource and information center for those who want to know more about children with learning disabilities (*Association for Children with Learning Disabilities*, 1973, pp. 26–27).

Parents are becoming our teachers. Most are eager to share. They offer to visit classrooms from kindergarten through graduate school. They let us into their homes. When we have been cruel, they restrain their impulse to hit back, and offer to help us understand. They do this for children. They do this because they understand that our ignorance can only hurt the ones they love.

REFERENCES

"Association for Children with Learning Disabilities," *The Exceptional Parent*, 3 (1973), 26–27.

FOSBURGH, L., "They Find Children in Need—and Ask Them to Join the Family," *New York Times*, January 22, 1974, p. 34.

GREENBERG, J., *A Child Called Noah*. New York: Holt, Rinehart and Winston, 1970.

HEISLER, V., *A Handicapped Child in the Family*. Grune & Stratton, 1972.

HERZ, H., "Eva, Child of Joy and Sorrow, in *If Your Child Is Handicapped*, ed. W. C. Kvaraceus and E. N. Hayes, pp. 109–30. Boston: Porter Sargent, 1969.

HOBBS, N., *The Futures of Children*. San Francisco: Jossey-Bass, 1975.

HOSEY, C., "Yes, Our Son Is Still With Us," *Children Today*, 2 (1973), 14–17, 36.

KASTEIN, S., and B. TRACE, *The Birth of Language*. Springfield, Ill.: Charles C Thomas, 1966.

KOVACS, D., " 'Josh': The Lonely Search for Help," *The Exceptional Parent,* 1 (1972), 29–30.

LINDE, T. F., AND T. KOPP, *Training Retarded Babies and Preschoolers.* Springfield, Ill.: Charles C. Thomas, 1973.

OUELLET, A. M., "Michelle: One Step At a Time," *The Exceptional Parent,* 4 (1974), 21–23.

PENDLER, B., "A Parent's View," *Children Today,* 4 (1975), 34–35.

RHODES, M. J., "Invisible Barrier," *The Exceptional Parent,* 1 (1972), 10–14.

ROBINSON, R., "Don't Speak to Us of Living Death," in *If Your Child Is Handicapped,* ed. W. C. Kvaraceus and E. N. Hayes, pp. 96–108. Boston: Porter Sargent, 1969.

SCHULTE-HILLEN, K. H., "My Search to Find the Drug that Crippled My Baby," in *If Your Child Is Handicapped,* ed. W. C. Kvaraceus and E. N. Hayes, pp. 37–52. Boston: Porter Sargent, 1969.

SULLIVAN, T., and D. GILL, *If You Could See What I Hear.* New York: Harper & Row, 1975.

THOMAS, L., "Karen Finds Love," *Ebony,* February 1974, pp 58–65.

ULRICH, S., *Elizabeth.* Ann Arbor: University of Michigan Press, 1972.

"Who Cares What Happens to Miriam?" *The Exceptional Parent,* 3 (1973), 11–17.

THREE

Growing Up Disabled

I received a telephone call. Mimi had died after open-heart surgery. The next day I went to the chapel. Mimi looked lovely but unreal. The real Mimi would never have been still for a minute. She would have been smiling at you, tugging at your sleeve, making friends, challenging anyone's indifference. She would have been jumping up and down, climbing steps, playing games, saying a definite "No!" to any request, but then usually doing it anyhow.

I had come with great hesitancy, remembering the hysteria and depression at the few funerals I had attended, my own father's and my favorite cousin's particularly. But there was no hysteria or depression at the chapel that Wednesday, only quiet grief and mourning for someone who was well-loved.

"She lived more in her four years than most people ever do," said her mother. "She took advantage of every minute she had. If we had put off the surgery any longer, she would have begun to deteriorate and to experience pain. I couldn't stand that thought."

"The doctors were marvelous. They worked for hours trying to save her. I've had some bad experiences with doctors, but this has changed my mind. She had the best possible care. They came to me afterwards and told me how sorry they were. I told them not to feel guilty. They had done their best, but some things are not in man's control."

"I know she had the best that she could have gotten in love, in education, in medical care. She leaves a void in our lives that will never be filled, but we know that she had the best possible life for her."

Near Mimi's casket was a huge floral wreath with the ribboned inscription "To Mimi Our Treasure, Mom, Dad, and Fluffy."

What is your impression of Mimi? I would venture to guess that you have formed a picture of her as a delicate but beautiful and joyous child, someone you would have wanted to know. She was that. But what if I had begun this story by telling you that Mimi was born not only with a congenital heart defect but also with Down's Syndrome, a condition commonly referred to as Mongolism? Would you still have felt this way? Or would you have vaguely pictured a heavy-set, flaccid child with a dull look whom you might feel sorry for but would not particularly want to know? This is, unfortunately, what often happens when we think of children in terms of labels. When a label carries information that stigmatizes, it may deprive us of the opportunity to experience the individuals behind the label. Because I wanted you to know and care about Mimi, I described her as an individual before I told you about how she was labeled.

In her brief life Mimi was happy. Whether she would have stayed happy had she lived to middle childhood or adolescence will remain an unanswered question. These periods would have brought new demands, expectations, and stresses. In fact, many mentally retarded or otherwise disabled children cannot negotiate the first four or five years of their lives successfully as Mimi did.

DEVELOPMENTAL PROCESSES AND THE SELF

Children begin to develop self-concepts in infancy as they learn to differentiate themselves from the outside world. They take delight in being able to do things with their fingers and hands and legs. They practice over and over again such ac-complishments as standing up and sitting down, grasping objects and letting go of them. Children learn about their environment too through this control over their bodies. During the first two years of life, the primary means of learning is action. Infants "study" objects by sucking them, by squeezing, poking, and pushing on them. During the course of physically acting upon their environments, infants begin to grasp cause and effect and begin to exhibit intentionality. The baby who accidentally hits a hanging rattle on several occasions while thrashing his legs soon begins to kick that rattle deliberately in order to see it swing and hear its sound. The infant who learns to direct his body movements in such a way as to cause desired effects in his environment begins to develop a sense of mastery.

Some disabled children have very limited potential for acting upon their environment in a physical way. The child with cerebral palsy may not have the muscular strength to creep, or may not be able to control the movements of his legs well enough to walk. He may have to lie in wait for someone to move him or to move part of the environment to him so that he can act upon it. Sometimes cerebral-palsied children do not have sufficient control over their hands to be able to use them effectively, and they may not be able to use speech or gestures to communicate what is of interest to them in their environment. Because of these physical limitations the young cerebral-palsied child may have a serious handicap in learning about his world and in developing a sense of mastery over it.

Other kinds of physical impairments may present special problems for the development of a sense of self in early life. The child who is a congenital amputee has no fingers to be counted, no hands to play pat-a-cake with, no arms with which to show affection. This is a double problem. First, the avenues by which the young child may learn about himself and his environment are limited. Second, the avenues by which he and his family can relate affectionately are reduced.

Physical disabilities may make the development of a sense of self more difficult, but so may mental disabilities. The severely retarded young child may not be able to make the discriminations basic to separating himself from his surroundings. He may not be able to learn, as most infants do, that these toes are his and are a part of him, in contrast to a rattle or a bottle which is not him. He may not learn easily that when he bites a toy he won't be hurt, but when he bites his hand, he will be. Such experiences help most infants come to understand what their physical self consists of. The severely retarded child may experience such pain over and over again without making the connection between his biting action and the pain he experiences when he acts on his foot or hand, but not when he acts on other things in his reach.

The autistic child presents a special problem in this regard. An infant of 15 or 18 months who sees his reflection in a mirror may not recognize himself. He may try over and over again to touch the child in the mirror. But by the age of 2 or 2½ most children recognize their mirrored reflections as images of their own selves. When I first introduced a full-length mirror into the classroom where I worked with severely disturbed children, the 6-year-old children who were labeled autistic tried to find the child in the mirror. Each tried to feel or grasp the child from the front of the mirror. After many fruitless attempts, they switched to searching for the child behind the mirror. Only after dozens of teaching experiences over a period of months did they come to recognize those children in the mirror as themselves.

The dictionary definition of autism is "the tendency to view life in terms of one's own needs and desires . . . unmindful of objective reality" (Random House Dictionary of the English Language, 1971, p. 100). Autistic children characteristically respond to people no differently than they do to inanimate objects. The human voice and the human face appear not to have any special attraction for these children, as they do for most other infants. Parents report that their young, autistic children appear to look through them instead of at them, that they can't establish eye contact, can't get any response from their children. Some parents report that their babies reject physical comforting, stiffen and scream when picked up. Mothering and fathering, including both their loving and instructional aspects, are two-way processes. Parents are stimulated to further parenting by the responses they get from their babies. When their babies don't respond, there is a breakdown in the normal self-stimulating process.

Raun is one of these children. Fortunately for him, his parents are special too. They were not turned off by this child who appeared not to see them. At 17 months Raun had already been labeled autistic. He rocked, and he spun things. There was "no communication by sound or gesture, no expression of wants, likes, or dislikes" (Kaufman, 1975, p. 43) Time was precious. Each day Raun became more encapsulated in his own world. Because they could find no treatment program for a 17-month-old autistic boy, Raun's parents created one for him. They bombarded him with stimulation, particularly human stimulation. They tickled and stroked him; hugged and talked to him; played peek-a-boo and body awareness games. They imitated his spinning, turning it into a communal event. Raun responded in small but sure ways. Real eye contact was established. He began to communicate his wants by cries and tugs. He began to speak. Autism does not go away, but this devastator of children can be tamed.

Who would you think would be more hampered in development during the first three years of life—children who cannot see or children who cannot hear? Most of us would say, with a fair amount of certainty, children who cannot see. This is true during the first one-and-a-half or two years of life. Seeing provides a major mode of information input. Even more important during this period is its role in guiding action. An infant's reaching and grasping is largely stimulated by the sight of something interesting. The muscle control and hand coordination that is developed by these activities come late to many blind children. The blind infant has little motivation for learning to hold up his head. Doing so does not enable him to experience a richer visual picture. For the same reason, sitting, standing, and walking may also be delayed.

Speech does not become a major tool for mediating experiences, for learning about the environment, until a child approaches the age of 2. With intact vision and motor control, the deaf child develops very much like a child without a hearing impairment during this early period. But somewhere before the end of the second year the picture begins to shift. Given parents who provide him with a modicum of opportunities for exploration, the blind child begins to catch up. He learns through touch and hearing, making better use of these senses than most children do. And he develops language.

There are many modes of communication. In our everyday lives all of us use gestures and signs. We nod, we point, we signal "stop." We communicate displeasure by a frown. We threaten with the shake of an extended index finger, and beckon with an inward curve of the same finger. We read people's feelings from the way they move and act. If our spouse is tired, he doesn't have to say so. We know from the way he stands and walks. But while we communicate feelings and some immediate needs by these nonverbal means, human beings rely overwhelmingly on speech as a means of communicating ideas, of passing on our culture, of extending our knowledge of all that is included in existence. The blind child shares this basic human tool. The young deaf child does not. He sees his mother's mouth move but it has no meaning to him. Never having heard the words of others, he has no awareness of the existence or meaning of words. While the 2-year-old blind child is beginning to be able to think about his experiences by using the words that stand for them, his deaf peer can only think about his experiences through images.

MOVING OUT INTO THE ENVIRONMENT

The preschooler wants to move out into his environment, to explore, to act upon it, to master its demands. He meets new adults, and becomes interested in other children. He begins to identify himself as an individual of a particular gender and the anatomy to prove it. He constantly tests his growing powers.

The disabled child may be vulnerable in many ways during this period. The deaf child may experience enormous frustration because of his limited ability to communicate. Babies are given nourishment, changed, bathed, and soothed regularly. They don't have to ask anyone to meet their basic needs. A lusty cry is an effective reminder to a tardy parent. But by the time a child is 3 his needs have grown beyond these few basic ones. The deaf child's mother may no longer be able to satisfy his cries or gestures by food, because what he may want is not food in a generic sense but rather a particular kind of food. If the child cannot make recognizably different sounds or gestures for ice cream, apple, salami, or any other food he desires, his appetite will often go unsatisfied. So will many of his other appetites including, often, his appetite for understanding what people are doing and why. In frustration, he may rage about, screaming, crying, and hitting out. It is not unusual for a deaf preschooler who has not yet acquired language to appear to be severely disturbed. Moreover, the deaf child's attempts to communicate will increasingly fail as he moves out into the larger world of hearing children and adults.

Parents are still the most significant others in the child's life at this time. Their attitudes and their behavior will influence strongly the way the disabled child feels about himself and the patterns of interaction that develop. Parents have the sometimes formidable job of helping their child to understand his disability, accept himself as he is, and find a satisfying way of expressing himself in his environment.

> I used to fantasize a little when I was a kid. And I used to dream. Dad used to tell me to pray really hard and anything will happen, anything's possible. So I would be just praying away at night — praying a miracle would happen and I would wake up and I would have arms and legs. I would pray and pray and wake up the next morning — and no arms and legs. ("Person to Person," 1973, p. 11)

> When my daughter first expressed apprehension about her lack of fingers, she seemed to think that they would grow in just as her teeth had. I could have let her go on thinking so, but eventually she would have realized that this was not true. I told her that she would not have any more fingers when she grew up, but that she would be able to do many things. . . . (Ouellet, 1972, pp. 32-33)

Parents must conquer their own apprehension of the special dangers that moving out into the environment holds for their child because of his disability. A mother of a blind child was in a constant state of panic once her daughter began to walk. This child made her way around by feeling. Foremost in the mother's mind was the possibility that her child would electrocute herself at a wall outlet. The child was never allowed out of her mother's reach until she entered school at age 5. As a result, her understanding of the environment was quite limited.

The dangers are real, just as they are for any young child, but even more so. In his autobiography, Harold Krents writes:

> My very first clear recollection is at the age of three running down the street far, far ahead of my mother and her two sisters. I thought I could outrace the wind . . . but inevitably I would deliver a devastating blow to a lamppost or parking meter with my forehead or my chin. I would go running back to my mother spitting blood and crying more from frustration than from pain.
>
> "How can you be so cruel?" my aunt would exclaim.
>
> "Do you think it's easy for me to let him go and hurt himself?" my mother replied. "The easiest thing in the world would be for me to always hold his hand, but I simply cannot do that. Someday there won't be someone to hold his hand, and he'll have to be able to make it in this world on his own. I want to prepare him for that. I not only want him to be independent, but I want him to love being that way." (Krents, 1972, p. 4)

The mother of a young deaf child tried to find a path that allowed her daughter to grow while providing her with reasonable protection.

> When Marsha was about four years old, we began to wonder what would happen if she got lost. . . . The possibility persisted in our minds. We had visions of the police trying to entertain a little deaf girl until we called to say we had lost one. So we decided that it would be wiser to take Marsha to the police station and introduce her. . . . The officers understood why we had come, Marsha responded to their friendliness and interest, and our mission was accomplished.
>
> In order to give Marsha a measure of freedom and still avoid too much anxiety, I started sewing name tapes in all of her outer garments. . . . In this way, she never leaves the house without some identification in her clothing. (Flaxman, 1955, pp. 163, 156)

Moving vehicles hold special dangers for the disabled child. The deaf child may be tempted to play in the street as other neighborhood children do, but he cannot hear the approach of vehicles that sends his playmates scurrying to the sidewalk. The blind child may be tempted to run to a friend who is calling to him from across the street. Since he does not *see* the area separating him from his friend, he may forget its special dangers.

The preschool years are a critical time in the child's development, a time in which the individual's style or basic patterns of interacting with his environment is formed. Some disabled children become persistent fighters for independence; others become demanding as well as dependent. Some use whatever senses are intact to avidly examine and learn about their environment; others withdraw into themselves. Some learn to use their disability to manipulate others. There are as many styles and patterns as there are disabled children. What the child becomes during this period is a combination of his basic constitutional characteristics—temperamental patterns, abilities, and disabilities—and what we have allowed or enabled him to do with them.

> My father was probably my only guiding light. . . . Right from the start he insisted that I face problems square on, no funny business, nothing. He told me what he thought I could do. He explained my handicap. . . . I was given specific duties around the house. . . . Bringing chairs in and out from dinner. . . . And I carried out the garbage. ("Person to Person," 1973, pp. 8–9)

The young man whose reminiscence you have just read is a quadruple amputee who uses prosthetic devices for arms and legs he never had. He was also a law student and a member of the National Board of Directors of the Easter Seal Society at the time he told this story.

THE MIDDLE YEARS

"Do you want to take the retard test?"
"Yes."
"What's the color of your hair?"

"Brown."

"What's the color of your dress?"

"Blue."

"What's the first thing I asked you?"

"The color of my hair."

"No. The first thing I asked you was if you wanted to take the retard test. You failed. You're a retard!"

This is an exchange that was endemic to the third and fourth grades of the New York City public school my daughter attended. It is a variation of a game that was being played ten and twenty and thirty years ago. My daughter reported it to me with obvious ambivalence. She knew it was something I wouldn't want her to say, but she wasn't quite ready to make an issue of it with her friends.

"That's not a good thing to say, you know."

"I know," she responded.

"Do you know why?"

"Because it makes people feel that they're not wanted."

During the middle years of childhood, from age 7 to 11 or 12, a large part of a child's life is spent in school. Real friendships develop, usually among children who are classmates, and peer values begin to challenge those of the parents. The child moves out into his community, going places and meeting people on his own. No longer can he or she be protected from all but a few select individuals. No longer can a loving mother make up for children who turn their backs. Unless he is severely retarded or disturbed, the child will sense how others perceive him, how they feel about him. If these reactions are consistently negative, they cannot help but affect the way the child thinks about himself and what he is willing to try. Even reactions other than rejection may confuse and hurt. A 12-year-old boy who was labeled mildly retarded related that he had always recognized his inability to do things as well as other children his age. While he was sometimes angry and resentful that this was so, he gained satisfaction from doing things as well as he could. His greatest disappointment did not come from failure, but from the artificial and dishonest responses of the people around him who were trying to be kind.

> They say: "What a nice drawing," when I know it isn't nice. . . . They say: "Boy, you almost caught that ball," when I know I missed it by a mile. They say: "How fast you run," when I know it isn't true. (Kapel, 1976, p. 42)

The years of middle childhood represent what could be called a stage of industry (Erikson, 1963). This is a period of skill development, a time when the child masters the basic tools he will need to function effectively in his society. In a sense, he becomes a worker, with school his place of work. The greatest danger during this period is that he will develop a sense of inferiority, a feeling that can come from either failure at skill development or rejection by his partners in skill development.

There is a child whose problem is more subtle than those we have been considering. His senses are intact and there is nothing wrong with his muscles. He wants to relate to people. His IQ is in the "normal" range—it may even be superior. Yet he often fails to develop a sense of industry, to master many of the tasks and skills expected of him, and to be accepted by his peers. For want of a better name, he is being called "learning disabled." Some of the other labels for him are "minimally brain damaged," "neurologically impaired," "hyperkinetic," "hyperactive," and "perceptually handicapped."

What is this child like? It's hard to say. Almost the only thing the experts agree upon is that there is a type of child who is different from most, who appears to have difficulties in certain areas, and who exasperates adults who try to teach or live with him. Characteristics that are commonly ascribed to him in the literature include: poor coordination; hyperactivity; perceptual-motor impairments; impulsiveness; short attention span; disorientation in time and space; problems in reading, writing, spelling, and speech.

His parents say:

We've tried everything and nothing works . . .

He can't sit still. He's on the move constantly . . .

He's got a hair-trigger temper . . .

He can't read and he's got an IQ of 124 . . .

I don't understand. Sometimes he can be so good . . .

Most of the time he acts like he just doesn't care . . .

You can never tell what might set him off . . .

When he leaves home he knows every spelling word perfectly and then he misses seven on the test . . .

It's hard for him to get started . . .

He's so disorganized! — He doesn't know where anything is . . .

He's got to know everything; he always wants to know "What's next?"

He gets everyone screaming at him . . .

He's not an easy child to live with. (Woodward and Biondo, 1972, pp. 13–18)

How many such children are there? The estimates of the percentage of children who are "learning disabled" range from 1 percent to 20 percent, depending upon the criteria used in making this judgment, as well as sociopolitical factors. Lower figures are used by funding agencies, those who want to push for an individualized approach to working with all children, and those who would like to minimize labeling. Higher figures are used by those who are pressing for additional funds for special services, parents of learning-disabled children, and those whose professional stature and security would be strengthened by such labeling. But whichever figure is used, these children exist and they need help if they are to avoid the development of a sense of inferiority. When learning disabled children talk about themselves, they say:

> I'm the dumbest kid in the class . . . Sometimes I can do it —
> sometimes I can't . . . I dunno — all of a sudden I'm naughty — I
> don't know why . . . Everyone says I'm smart enough — I don't
> know why I can't . . . Other kids don't have this problem. Why is
> it so hard for me? . . . (Ibid., pp. 26–28)

When I was 7 or 8, there was a big boy who used to sometimes play with us. He was always dressed in a checked cap and he carried his knitting with him in a shopping bag. No one knew how old he was but he always wanted to play with the young children. Sometimes the children mocked him, but we liked him too. He was funny and fun to be with. Then one day he stopped coming around. We asked for him and found out that he had died. He hadn't been a boy, either. He was 47 at the time of his death. He was Mongoloid. In order to gain some kind of acceptance outside his immediate family, he had become a clown and mascot to the children of the block.

Unfortunately, this is not just a story from long ago. It is something that is still happening today as children with disabilities find that many of their peers will not accept them as they are. Some become clowns; some try to buy friendship with possessions; some withdraw into the small circle of their disabled classmates; others find that they can gain acceptance only from those who are their juniors.

Mary Ann was 9. She went to a special school for the deaf that was about a twenty-minute drive from her home. None of the children from her class lived near her, because they came from all parts of the city. Mary Ann had two friends. One was her 5½-year-old cousin. The other was a 5-year-old girl who lived down the street. These two children were happy that someone so much bigger and in many ways so much more skilled would play with them. Mary Ann fixed her cousin's hair, and made clothes for her dolls. She taught the little girl down the street how to play ball and how to use a pogo stick. But while Mary Ann could do all these things, could jump rope and roller skate and ride a bike and play jacks, not one of the 7- or 8- or 9-year-old girls from the block would play with her.

Mary Ann's problem is common to most deaf children who cannot learn to speak clearly. Unless one listens carefully and gets used to the indistinct diction, poor phrasing, and odd inflectional patterns, the speech of deaf children may sound strange and impossible to understand. Most hearing children don't get past an initial exposure. Mary Ann could communicate well by signs. But while this skill enabled her to speak to other deaf persons, it was a useless aid in acquiring friends in the hearing world.

A fourth-grade boy writes:

A Handycap Person

When I was in camp their was a girl on my bus. Her name was Jill. She could not hear or talk. On the bus she made funny sounds and looked funny but I don't think she liked it. A lot of kids made her cry because they made fun of her. One time a kid punched her in the teeth. ("A Handycap Person," 1973)

Over and over again I hear stories from saddened parents about how their disabled children have lost their neighborhood friends after the preschool years. Undoubtedly the fact that disabled children often go to schools different from their neighbors contributes to this isolation. So does the stigma attached to being in a special class in the local public school. So does the fact that there may be an increasing gap between the kinds of things that disabled children and their nondisabled peers can do. But there appears to be something more even than this. The middle years bring with them a kind of exclusivity or cliquishness. The disabled child often finds himself a member of the out-group.

At age 7, Harold Krents was in a regular second-grade class. He had no trouble mastering the academic work, but when he tried to join his male classmates in a battle against the girls he was told clearly that he was not a member of their group.

"What are you doing here?" one rather large recruit asked.

"I've come to fight with you," I replied.

"We don't want you," said the entire army of boys.

I stood there in stunned disbelief.

"Why not?" I asked angrily, "I'm a boy."

"Yes, but you're blind," said the large recruit.

"Only some," I said defensively.

"You are blind," he repeated. The way he said it made me flinch.

"I'm a boy first and blind second," I said quietly.

"No, you're not, you're a blind boy."

For some reason, the entire army of the boys found this very amusing, and raucous laughter reverberated through the playground. (Krents, 1972, p. 63)

For the orthopedically impaired child, the opportunities for peer socialization may be severely limited because of problems of mobility. There are many places a child in a wheelchair can't go. These may include the homes of some of the neighborhood children, unless a parent is available to carry the child and carry his wheelchair. Mobility is important to the play of children in the middle years, both to its content and organization. Eight-year-olds roller skate and play ball. They go places on their bikes. They may begin playing at John's house and suddenly decide to switch to Ruth's. Even when accepted by other children in the neighborhood, the child who walks with the help of crutches and braces, or who moves slowly with braces, often can't keep up. If your friends are jumping rope, you can be a turner. If your friends are playing punch ball, you can keep score and be the umpire. But when your friends hop on their bikes and take off for the playground, there's no place for you.

ADOLESCENCE

All teenagers worry, Jamie. And the teenager with a disability is no exception—only he has more to worry about. He too worries about being accepted, and he worries about his future. However, he is also sensitive about his physical defects. For you, the bladder and bowels are a source of great humiliation. Even when these problems are solved by catheters, you still fear having an "accident." . . . It takes time to overcome the embarrassment and fear of being laughed at. But you cannot hide from the world, Jamie, if you are to grow up to be a well-adjusted adult. . . . I have *adjusted* to my disability and my adolescent years were spent *learning* to adjust. And believe me, it wasn't easy. . . . I cried a lot as a teenager. (Helton, 1974, p. 5)

So wrote an adult with spina bifida to a young girl with the same problem. Spina bifida is a congenital spinal cord injury resulting from incomplete closure of the lower spine. It often results in paralysis of legs, and lack of bladder and bowel control. Until recently, the two to four children per 1,000 who were born with spina bifida rarely lived into late adolescence, much less adulthood. If they survived the first days of life and the dozens of surgical operations needed to improve their health and mobility, they often died from renal failure due to a history of urinary infections. A good part of their short lives were spent in hospitals, and their education came largely from hospital-based teachers or teachers who provided home instruction. Contacts with peers outside the family or hospital were almost nonexistent.

Today, with improved drug treatment and surgical procedures, the story is different. Children with spina bifida are surviving. (There are approximately 100,000 persons with spina bifida living in the United States.) They are going to school. They are learning work skills. While all kinds of procedures and equipment have been devised to minimize the medical and social problems created by their disability, the adolescent with spina bifida must deal with the existential aspect of his impairments himself.

The beginning of adolescence was painful for Rita. She was 13 and in the eighth grade. She had never been labelled handicapped, but there had always been something different about her. The children on the block had noticed it. There was a kind of awkwardness about her movements. She clumped down the street as if she weighed 200 pounds. She never really learned to skip and she was terrible at any of the games the children played during recess. There was something strange about the way she acted too. She asked questions about things anyone would be expected to know. When she entered junior high school, matters took a turn for the worse. Whereas she had been able to find one or two children to play with her occasionally before, there was no one now.

Thirteen-year-old girls spend their non-school, non-homework hours talking about boys, experimenting with makeup, moving to music, worrying about their clothes and figures, getting crushes. In all of these experiences Rita was out of place. She couldn't get the dance movements right. An experiment with her mother's makeup resulted in a clownlike appearance which Rita did not recognize as such. The wiles and intrigues of 13-year-old girls who are beginning to think of boys in sexual terms were as hard for her to grasp as Russian or Chinese would have been. Almost every time I saw her she was crying or obviously had been crying.

The last time I saw Rita she was in a candy store with her mother. This girl, who could read a seventh- or eight-grade book, picked out a candy bar from the counter display and asked the proprietor, "Is this candy free?" Rita was completely serious, and she couldn't understand why her mother was so upset by this question. Rita doesn't live at home any more. I don't know where she is. Someplace where people will help, I hope.

There is an aspect of socialization, of coming to understand the mores of our society, which most of us learn through general exposure. We watch older siblings and babysitters and parents doing things, and we imitate or model ourselves after them. We integrate our various experiences and come out with unwritten, even nonverbal, generalizations about what is appropriate and what isn't. Learning-disabled or neurologically impaired persons like Rita don't learn well in this unsystematized way. Their integrative abilities are poor. They can't put things together for themselves. During adolescence they flounder about, not really understanding why they are loners, nor why they are often a source of irritation to their teachers and anxiety to their parents.

Late adolescence is a time of anticipation, of planning, of anxiety. What will I become? Can I make it in the nondisabled world? Will I be accepted into college? Will I be able to keep up with the work there or will it be too much for me? Can I find any employer who will take a chance on me? Will I be able to hold onto a job? Will I be able to travel independently? Will I continue to make too many stupid mistakes? Will anyone want to marry me? Will I be able to have children? Will I be able to take care of them? Will my children resent having a disabled parent? Is the future worth the constant struggle?

REFERENCES

BAUER, J., "A Handycap Person," composition by a fourth-grade boy, 1973.

FLAXMAN, G. (Dr.), and G. FLAXMAN, "Growing Up With Marsha," in *If Your Child Is Handicapped*, ed. W. C. Kvaraceus and E. N. Hayes, pp. 148-66. Boston: Porter Sargent, 1969.

HELTON, S., "Dear Jamie," *Exceptional Parent*, 4 (1974), 5-11.

KAPEL, S. (M.D.), "Handicapped Boy Cites Peeves," *New York Daily News*, January 13, 1976, p. 42.

KAUFMAN, B., "Reaching the "Unreachable" Child," *New York Magazine*, February 3, 1974, pp. 43-49.

KRENTS, H., *To Race the Wind*. New York: Putnam, 1972.

OUELLET, A. M., "Michelle: A Long Way to Kindergarten," *The Exceptional Parent,* 2, no. 1 (1972), 31-33.

"Person to Person," *The Exceptional Parent,* 3, no. 2 (1973), 7-12.

Random House Dictionary of the English Language, unabridged ed. New York: Random House, 1971.

WOODWARD, D., and N. BIONDO, *Living Around the Now Child.* Columbus, Ohio: Merrill, 1972.

FOUR

On Being a Disabled Adult

We wanted to get engaged, and we went to the warden, and we were told it would be okay as long as we understood that we couldn't get married. We've been engaged ten years now.*

These are the words of a woman with cerebral palsy who lived in a residential center in England. Neither she nor her fiancé could care for themselves independently. The staff people of the institution were helpful and friendly. There were no horrors such as have been uncovered recently at some of our own American institutions. But marriage, no. Sex, no. Those were reserved for normal people.

Probably the most important need for most people, disabled or not, is that of feeling a human bond—belonging, having people to share with, being part of the human experience. For the disabled, particularly those whose minds are intact but whose bodies are not, the satisfaction of this need may present

*From *Like Other People* (16 mm film), distributed by Perennial Education. Northfield, Ill., 1973.

serious problems. A young woman with severe impairment resulting from cerebral palsy, typing by use of a stick projected from a helmet, writes:

> But it is vitally necessary that the severely handicapped person attempt to form a few really close and binding friendships with people who both understand him as a person and also comprehend the full significance of his disability or handicap, to whom he can easily and frankly vent the turbulent feelings about life situations which he must confront. Without such two-way, free-flowing relationships, one feels horribly shut off and lonely—and life soon becomes meaningless alone. (Sutherland, 1968, p. 29)

Disabilities in adults, as in children, range from the subtle to the obvious, from minor impairments which hardly handicap to those which affect multiple functions severely. The popular literature contains frequent references to Leonardo da Vinci's mirror writing as well as his inability to learn Latin, a sine qua non for educated people in his time, in spite of his obvious brilliance. Abraham Lincoln's headaches and melancholy outlook have been interpreted as a reflection of an undiagnosed visual impairment.

> "His problem was recorded for posterity pictorially, as well as in accounts from the period," Dr. Steinberg said. "In the paintings, he appears to be looking at you with one eye and away from you with the other eye. The position of anatomical rest for one eye was higher than for the other eye."

> This brings about a double vision which is inacceptable to the organism. All efforts are then brought into play, every bit of neuromuscular control to overcome, to compensate, to eliminate the double vision. . . . He compensated for nature's imperfection (to align the different images from the two eyes). . . . He suffered excruciating headaches as a result.[1]

---

[1] A. Murray, "Hope for 'Lincoln's Complaint,' " *New York Times*, February 11, 1973, pp. 71, 88. © 1973 by The New York Times Company. Reprinted by permission.

DEPENDENCE AND INDEPENDENCE

The major task facing the disabled adult is to establish independence. Independence has different meanings. For the adult whose only impairment is a visual loss, a hearing loss, or mild retardation, independence may mean exactly what it means to nonhandicapped adults: economic, physical, and social self-sufficiency. To those with severe physical or mental impairments, to those with impairments of multiple senses, independence may not mean quite the same thing.

Alice was a 26-year-old brain-injured woman living in a group home, attending a sheltered workshop and spending weekends and holidays with her parents. Things were going fairly smoothly. A young, enthusiastic professional felt that Alice could be more independent. He arranged for her and two other women from the workshop to move into their own apartment. From the first day of this move her parents noticed changes.

> We visited her on Saturday and she wasn't her usual self at all. She was snappy to us and swore at us—she had never done that before. She said that one of her roommates was mean and was bugging her. And she didn't think Mr. Park liked her either.
>
> We talked to Mr. Park and he said she was just feeling her oats and exaggerating her independence because we had protected her for so long.
>
> On Wednesday afternoon they called us from the workshop. Alice had been crying all day. . . .
>
> One Friday, they called us again and said we'd better come and get her. She hadn't shown up at the workshop, so they sent someone over to the apartment. She was uncontrollable. We saw the psychiatrist that afternoon, and he recommended that we put her in the psychiatric ward of the county hospital because she might hurt herself. ("Independence?" 1974, pp. 41–42)

Alice looked like everyone else. It was hard to believe that she couldn't take care of herself. Other persons with disabilities are assumed by almost all of us to be unable to do so. Robert Smithdas is deaf and blind. So is his wife Michelle. They communicate by using the manual alphabet to spell words into each other's hands. When Robert Smithdas is not busy with his work as director of community education at the National Center for Deaf-Blind Youths and Adults in Long Island, and when Michelle Smithdas is not busy with her work as a teacher's aide at the same center, they can be found in their apartment, where Mr. Smithdas cooks French, Spanish, and Chinese dishes for guests (Fields, 1976, p. 42).

Robert Smithdas is exceptional. Most deaf-blind individuals can be taught basic self-care and mobility, but few can match his achievements of mind, of profession, or of functional living skills. However, many blind individuals whose hearing is not impaired can attain independence in everyday living. The blind can learn to travel, to play ball, to dance, to cook, to take care of their young children. They can tell time, play chess, apply makeup, bowl, and do carpentry work. There are excellent programs for training blind children and adults in independent living.

Ideas for Better Living (1974-75), a catalogue of special aids for the blind distributed by the American Foundation for the Blind, is fascinating reading. In it one can find such games as scrabble, monopoly, checkers, and backgammon adapted for the blind. Raised outlines and recesses define playing areas. Shape replaces color in defining which checkers belong to which player. Braille symbols are used in place of letters, and dice have raised dots instead of flat ones. The catalogue also contains watches whose covers open at the press of a button, allowing a blind person to tell the time by feeling the position of the hands in relation to the Braille numbers. An assortment of adapted timers, tape measures, body thermometers, bathroom scales, padlocks, directional compasses, and cooking aids can also be found in the catalogue.

Blindness is becoming increasingly a problem of adulthood, usually advanced adulthood, and often a side effect of such diseases as diabetes. Retrolental fibroplasia, once a major source of blindness in children, and one that was a direct result of medical efforts to sustain life in premature babies, has been eliminated. No longer are infants treated with doses of oxygen large enough to damage the retinas of their eyes.

Other causes of blindness are now correctable by newer surgical procedures. Thus more and more, training of the blind means training adults who once had vision to live without it. Can you cross the street safely without the information your eyes give you? Not likely. Could you learn to do so if you lost your vision? Most likely, yes. You would be trained to listen to the sounds of traffic and understand what they mean. When vehicles on the street parallel to you start up and those perpendicular to you stop, you are facing a green light. By using your cane to avoid bumping into obstacles that may be in your path, and by continuing alertness to changes in traffic sounds, you would be able to cross independently and safely. Before even getting to the task of crossing streets you would have gone through a major part of a course on orientation and mobility training, a course designed to train the senses, develop self-confidence, master the use of human guides and long canes, build skills in orienting oneself and moving about in indoor and outdoor environments. You would learn to orient yourself in familiar places by the use of landmarks; to trail your hand along "shorelines" like walls or hedges; to use the hand and forearm technique to avoid bumping into such things as partially open doors; to anticipate stairs by recognizing voice sounds at different levels and by recognizing the sound of ascending footsteps. You would learn to ask for help when you need it (*How Does a Blind Person Get Around?*, 1975).

How do you light a match safely if you're blind; or use a sharp knife; or pour milk into coffee without spilling over the top of the cup? These things too you can be taught in a rehabilitation center for the blind. There are some things, though, that others

feasible as we enter middle to late adolescence, the period when such choices and the preparation toward making them realistic begins. For many persons with disabilities this is not the case.

A disability may interfere directly with the individual's ability to perform basic work tasks. A deaf woman may be an excellent typist but her inability to respond to telephone calls would prevent her from serving effectively as a "gal Friday." Similarly, a blind person would be directly and obviously handicapped as a salesperson for cosmetics or any other item for which color selection is central. A considerable number ˆ ĵobs are eliminated as possible occupational choices for pҽ   with disabilities because their impairments prevent them frҽ   ҽerforming basic work tasks. Sometimes, this must be. Sometimҽ it need not be. In a one-secretary office, the secretary must perform a variety of tasks, but in large offices there can be typists and telephone operators and receptionists. This concept of specialization has made it possible for more persons with disabilities to obtain work. Extension of this concept would make many more occupational choices available to competent persons with disabilities, at little or no additional cost to anyone.

The TV program "Ironside" was kind of a joke. What police department would allow such irregularities, make such adjustments to fit the special needs of a wheelchair-bound cop? Ironside was not a person with a disability, he was a superperson—so super, in fact, that his department could not function without him. But let's look at the real situation for a moment. Does a physical disability make a person unfit for all police work? It may well make a person unfit to be a patrolman or even a detective, but are there not aspects of police work that involve minds, voices, and hands, but not legs? Not only should it be possible for some disabled policemen to be retained, and retrained, but it should be possible to hire persons who are already disabled. What this would require would be the flexibility to feel, think, and organize in new ways. With more flexibility in our thinking we could make many jobs open to persons with disabilities in schools, churches, banks, department stores, and many other places of employment.

> For *today's* disabled adults, let us take a deliberate look at every job opportunity around us—at home, at work, on the way to work, everywhere—and ask whether a disabled person could do that job.

> Think carefully, and ask yourself what each job entails. What *abilities* are essential? What disabilities are actually irrelevant? . . . The inability to walk need not make one ineligible for employment as a receptionist, bank teller or secretary. . . . While we cannot deny specific disabilities, we can ask: Would it be acceptable if this task were performed more slowly? . . . Or could adaptive equipment be developed to enable a disabled person to perform given tasks? The point is that we can begin to consider occupations systematically from this perspective. ("Change the Future Now," 1975, p. 5)

Mark Swerdloff lost his legs after a car smashed him against his own stalled vehicle. The dental career he had planned appeared to be lost until one of his classmates designed a completely hand-operated unit for him. With this unit Dr. Swerdloff can perform all dental functions from his wheelchair. From this wheelchair he completed his dental education with top honors. From this wheelchair he instructs his students in oral surgery at The School of Dental Medicine of the State University of New York at Stony Brook (Fields, 1975, p. 60).

There are other adjustments we could make that would cost money. A blind executive may need more secretarial help than a sighted one, for there will be written materials that will have to be read to him and there may be occasions when a secretary-reader will have to accompany him on business trips. A deaf person in a hearing, verbal environment may sometimes need the services of an interpreter who "signs," or may need a stenographer to record and transcribe a presentation he could not lip-read sufficiently well. A person with a severe physical disability may need some assistance in travel.

Who assumes these costs? Occasionally private employers do. Occasionally the disabled person pays for these services himself. Occasionally organizations for the disabled can help. Federal government agencies that hire disabled workers sometimes provide such services. Supportive *equipment* is, in the long run, much less expensive than human support services. As technology advances, fewer human support services will be needed. The blind executive will do his own "reading" with the aid of a computer which almost instantaneously translates the printed word into a spoken one. Undoubtedly, compact computerized machines will be designed to do the reverse for deaf persons—i.e., translate oral presentations into printed manuscripts. Electric wheelchairs with mechanical braces operated by the tongue will enable quadraplegics to write. State rehabilitation services, which receive much of their funding from the federal government, usually assume financial responsibility for the special materials and equipment disabled persons need in carrying out their work.

The Rehabilitation Act of 1973 extended civil rights to the disabled in the area of employment. Since January 1974 any firm having federal contracts in excess of $2,500—an estimated half of all business enterprises in the country—has had to develop affirmative action plans for employment of the handicapped. Employers must further demonstrate a willingness to make reasonable accommodations in relation to a person's disability. The federal government itself has become a major employer of the disabled. Deaf persons are employed as distribution clerks for the U.S. Postal Service, where their inability to hear keeps them from being bothered by the consistently high noise levels under which they work. Blind persons are employed by the Internal Revenue Service to answer taxpayers' questions. At their fingertips as they work is a book of tax laws and guidelines in Braille. Many state governments have also instituted programs for hiring the handicapped. Progress is being made, but slowly, too slowly for hundreds of thousands of persons with disabilities. Some of these persons are veterans of the Vietnam War, which left

320,000 men disabled (" 'New Deal' for Handicapped in Jobs, Housing, Recreation . . .," 1974). Many of them still wait, jobless and with little hope.

Any support that we, in the person of our government, give to make employment of the disabled feasible more than pays for itself. It means that persons who might otherwise have been dependent upon social security payments for a lifetime can pay their own way and even return money in the form of income taxes. But we are shortsighted and often defeat our own purposes along with the meaningfulness of the disabled person's existence.

> I worked three years for the Nassau County Department of Social Services and was forced to resign to qualify for Medicaid because I need a home health aid. Although I am incapable of in-dependently performing any activities of daily living, I was declared "not disabled" by state and federal law because I **earned** over $140 per month and worked full time. . . . Aides cost from $25-35 per day, and I had rent, utilities, car, and food expenses. Instead of partially helping me, they forced me to stop working and go on total assistance. (Panzarino, 1974, p. 14)

Disabilities eliminate certain job possibilities. Economic considerations and rigidities of thinking limit opportunities for other positions. But by far the most limiting factors involved in job opportunities available to the disabled are attitudes. Employers and co-workers feel uncomfortable, don't want to get involved, don't want the responsibility, don't believe disabled persons can do the work and aren't willing to put them to the test. In spite of having had the highest scholastic average in his class at Columbia University School of Dental and Oral Surgery, and in spite of having completed a residency in oral surgery, it took Mark Swerdloff five months to find a job.

Even when employers are receptive, the path is sometimes rocky. There have been three major national projects to train and place retarded individuals, one an industrial laundry pro-ject, another a federal government project, and the third a pro-ject operated by the National Association for Retarded Citizens

(NARC). In both the industrial laundry project and the project operated by NARC, which involved restaurant jobs, slightly over a third of the trainees were dropped during the first ten weeks of training because of adjustment problems (The President's Committee on Mental Retardation and The President's Committee on Employment of the Handicapped, 1974).

Donald is a mildly retarded young man who obtained work as a mail clerk with the W. T. Grant Company, which had a long-established policy of favoring employment of the retarded. For two years before he had been hired by Grant's, he had been unable to hold a job for more than a brief time. Donald got off to a good start. He quickly learned to load the office truck and deliver the mail to the building's twenty floors. After two months he received a raise. Seven more raises were to follow during the next six-year period. But Donald's continuing employment was as much a reflection of his father's constant involvement as it was of Donald's performance.

> Any other employer would have dismissed Donald. There have been some excruciating episodes during the past six years. Scarcely a day has passed when we have not prayed that Grant would understand and that our son would come to accept the position of mail clerk as one for which he is suited. . . . (Hurwitz, 1973, p. 144)

Donald wasn't satisfied with his position as a mail delivery clerk at Grant's. He aspired to be a bookkeeping machine operator, a position that was considered beyond his abilities. If he couldn't get promoted at Grant's, he wanted to become an ambulance driver. But Donald had failed a driving test after months of practice. Or he wanted to be a bank teller, but no bank was likely to hire a retarded person for that position. He needed a better background in arithmetic, he was told after an interview. When Donald couldn't obtain another position at Grant's, he became irritable at work, cursing, muttering to himself, and screaming that he did not have to work in a mailroom all his life. Donald was accurately reflecting our cultural ethos. To be successful means to get ahead at work, to get a higher-status job. In Donald's case it didn't fit.

On the other hand, persons with disabilities have good work records. They are reliable. Their absentee rate is low and they don't give up jobs as often as the nondisabled. For some jobs, they may be the workers of choice. Those retarded individuals who did get through the training period in the three major national projects mentioned earlier received excellent work ratings.

How do you get to work if your legs or arms don't work, or if you don't have legs or arms? Here we are witness to the marvelous ingenuity of the human mind. Cars have been adapted with hand controls that can be operated not only by paraplegics but even by quadriplegics who have only limited use of their upper limbs. Norma Milam drives to work using her feet.

> It was a present from 37 prisoners. Norma was born without arms. She had graduated from Emory and Henry College with a B.A. in sociology, and she had a thirst for independence. A drafting instructor at Virginia State Prison knew of this thirst because Norma had been his wife's classmate. He began to think of a van with specially designed foot controls. Thirty-seven prisoners became interested too. They raised $9,000 for such a van by working at the 1973 Virginia State Fair. Using her left leg and foot to steer, and her right foot to control the brake and accelerator, Norma passed her driving test on the first try. Everyday she drives to a veteran's administration hospital where she works as a vocational rehabilitation specialist. (Haynes, 1974).

Norma Milam illustrates another trend in regard to employment of persons with disabilities. Traditionally, vocational rehabilitation counselors have not been disabled themselves or have had relatively minor disabilities. Today, increasingly, rehabilitation specialists who work with the disabled are themselves persons with disabilities, often severe ones. This serves two purposes. Clearly, it opens up new jobs for the disabled, but equally important is what it says to disabled clients: "You are no more disabled than I am, probably less. Yet look at me. I have made it. I have a purpose. I am making a contribution. You can too."

LOVE, SEX, MARRIAGE, PARENTHOOD

During his second year, he and Janice were together everywhere, and together they ruined all the attempts the school made to put them out of each other's way. They found forgotten windows and unused storage rooms. Most of all they used their deafness. They were all and completely mute; they understood nothing, they agreed to everything. They nodded and smiled and said yes to everyone, teacher, matron and master; they promised to reform and then went where they wished. In April they ran away together. Outside. They found a church like one Abel knew at home. When the minister saw what they wanted and that they were deaf, he wrote another man's name on a paper for them and so they were directed to a Justice of the Peace, who married them without questions—for four times the usual fee. (Greenberg, 1970, p. 24)

In this moving novel, Joanne Greenberg depicts the strangeness of "Outside" for a deaf couple. Janice had spent all of her growing years in a residential school for the deaf. Abel had spent his on an isolated farm and then in that same school for the deaf. "Outside" was the world of the hearing—alluring, fascinating, and puzzling. For Janice and Abel it became also a nightmare, heavy with punishment for a crime they didn't understand. After their daughter Margaret was born it was she who interpreted "Outside" to them, who negotiated with it, who was their voice. Margaret paid a heavy price for her parents' deafness.

The people in Joanne Greenberg's novel spent their developmental years as many deaf people did in the past, in isolated residential schools, being with their families only for brief snatches, unprepared for life in a hearing world. Today deaf children, particularly those from urban areas, increasingly live at home and attend special day schools. A smaller number attend neighborhood schools. "Outside" will be less dangerous for these children.

People with disabilities have normal children and they have children with disabilities. Some couples with disabilities have a higher probability of giving birth to children with similar impairments. Genetic counseling is now at the point at which probabilities of occurrence of disabilities in children can often be given with a fair amount of certainty.

The Hliboks wanted four children and they had four. All six Hliboks are deaf, but their lives are full. "Outside" holds no strangeness for them. The three school-age children in the family attend regular schools. The baby still attends the Lexington School for the Deaf, as the three other children did, to receive training in lip-reading and speech. Even at Lexington the pre-school and lower-grade classes are integrated, with many hearing children from the neighborhood in attendance. Mr. Hlibok works for a firm of engineering consultants. Mrs. Hlibok participates in organizations attached to a neighborhood church. Mr. and Mrs. Hlibok are convinced that they can give their children enough love and security to make up for a lack of hearing.[3]

Laugh with Accent (Cheever and Cheever, 1975) is a book of cartoons that laughs at disability. It was designed primarily for persons with disabilities, and the cartoons were culled from *Accent On Living,* a magazine devoted to serving this population, and in particular the physically handicapped. As the dedication states: "If you're able to laugh at yourself, to accept your disability, others will accept it too." This book contains 100 cartoons within its covers and another 6 on its covers. Over 10 percent of these cartoons deal with sex. The point made by most of these cartoons, as in the examples provided, is that a physical

---

[3]V. L. Warren, "They're All Deaf But, as a Family, They Don't Feel Handicapped," *New York Times,* October 3, 1973, p. 34. © 1973 by The New York Times Company. Reprinted by permission.

disability doesn't turn an individual into an asexual person. Physically disabled persons do have special feelings for members of the opposite sex; many can have sexual relations; many can start new life.

"Don't come all unglued — I'm just here to keep you calmed down."

Figure 4-1 SOURCE: R.C. Cheever and G. C. Cheever, eds., *Laugh with Accent.* Bloomington: Accent Special Publications, 1975, p. 26. Reprinted with permission. Copyright 1975, ACCENT On Living, Inc.

While disabled persons marry others with disabilities, disabled persons also date and marry nondisabled individuals.

> Some guys are afraid to ask me out because they don't know what to do with my wheelchair . . . but the majority of guys don't think much of it.

It's no big thing to ask an able-bodied girl for a date. You don't just go up to any girl and ask her out. You get to know her and you can tell how she feels about you and your condition and then you decide whether or not to ask her for a date. If two people like one another's company, a wheelchair won't make any difference. You just throw it in the trunk or the back seat. ("I Was Afraid to Come to College . . . But Then I Met a Guy in a Wheelchair . . ., 1975, pp. 42–43)

"And **this** one is for group therapy!"

Figure 4-2 SOURCE: R.C. Cheever and G. C. Cheever, eds., *Laugh with Accent.* Bloomington: Accent Special Publications, p. 29. Reprinted with permission. Copyright 1975, ACCENT On Living, Inc.

Margaret and John Lester were engaged before the car accident.

"I can't stand it," said Margaret. "I just don't know whether we're engaged or unengaged. John doesn't seem to want to discuss it."

"I think you'd better send him to me," said the doctor. "I'd like a word with him, in any case."

In his office he gave the young man a clear and concise picture of Margaret's condition. "She will never walk on her feet again, she will always be susceptible to skin breakdowns due to pressure, and to serious bladder infections. These are the bane of every paraplegic—they can lead to disaster or even death; only with scrupulous, unremitting care can they be avoided. We think we can teach some limited control of bodily functions. . . . Now, on the positive side, there are plenty of things people can do from a wheelchair. . . . Motherhood is also possible in many cases."

"In Margaret's case?"

"I would say so."

There was a silence. Dr. Cheshire leaned forward, and said with great intensity, "Look, if you are going to break off your engagement, for God's sake go in there and do it *now*, not in six months' time."

"What I can't understand," said John, "is how we are going to cope with the problems of the day-to-day living."

"Then I suggest you stay around and observe the rehabilitation training given by our staff . . . But you haven't answered my question."

"What question?"

"The question as to whether or not you still contemplate marriage. I have a right to ask you because Margaret is my patient, and her well-being is my concern."

John stared at the doctor in great surprise. "But it's never occurred to me that we'd do anything else except go straight on with our plans. Of course we're going to get married! I'm merely trying to find out how on earth we're going to manage all the practical side of things."[4]

Fred Fay is a quadriplegic. His wife is a paraplegic. Their young son is not disabled. This presents no problem to them but it does to many others.

> But we get the most incredible reactions from other people about how can you discipline him, who do you have take care of him, what do you do when he hides in the closet or runs out of reach and you want to spank him? Just unreal reactions from otherwise intelligent people. They think that because we are disabled that we are completely incompetent parents. ("Person to Person," part III, 1973, p. 74)

How do you manage if a wheelchair is your only means of mobility? Not easily, particularly if your home is designed for a person who can stand and walk; particularly if you don't want or can't get help.

> Her own personal toilet routines took endless time in the inconvenient house. Now she had also to cope with the demands of a hungry and incontinent little new-comer. She could get the wheelchair neither into the laundry to do the washing nor outside to hang it up. She had to manage with a hand basin. . . . Sterilizing the bottles was a nightmare when one had to lean precariously from a wheelchair and manage heavy saucepans of boiling water on a stove which was exactly the wrong height. . . . Bathing Cindy became a main problem; Margaret couldn't balance well enough to lean over and fill the baby-bath from the bathroom taps. It had to be filled slowly and carefully at the cold tap in the kitchen, and the murderous hot water added to it from the kettle. Then she would carry it on her lap to the dining-room table, wheeling carefully so that it wouldn't slop over. Sometimes she almost panicked and longed for someone to take over. . . .[5]

[4]From *Mermaid on Wheels: The Remarkable Story of Margaret Lester,* by June Epstein, pp. 54–55. (New York: Taplinger, 1969; Sydney: Ure Smith). Copyright © 1967 by June Epstein. Reprinted with permission.

[5]From *Mermaid on Wheels: The Remarkable Story of Margaret Lester,* by June Epstein, p. 137. (New York: Taplinger, 1969; Australia: Ure Smith). Copyright © 1967 by June Epstein. Reprinted with permission.

A few years later in a new house equipped to meet her needs, Margaret Lester tended her two young children competently while awaiting the birth of her third child. Now she was able to say, "Management of babies is quite easy from a wheelchair." As for when the children get older, "Children whose mothers are disabled learn to wash and dress themselves, go shopping and take telephone messages at a very early age. . . . In a wheelchair you can handle all household duties, but there is a time limit. You simply take much longer to care for yourself and the family."[6]

SELF-ACTUALIZATION

For many years the focus of personality studies by psychologists was psychopathology. Today there is another growing area of study, that of individuals who can be called competent, self-actualizing, healthy, or creative. Psychologists could learn much about self-actualization through a study of selected persons with disabilities. It is hard enough for human beings who have the good fortune of intact bodies and minds to live fully. The person with a disability who does this has won a more difficult battle. He has met not only the challenges we all face in making our way through life but also the existential confrontation with himself over his impaired state.

Psychologists might study Henry Viscardi, Jr., who was born with two stumps instead of legs; who spent his first seven years in a hospital; who stood 3 feet 8 inches tall until he was 27 years old when he received his first pair of artificial legs. He can be reached at the Human Resources Center in Albertson, Long Island, where 200 severely disabled adults who were considered unemployable are now working, some in electronics assembly, some in data processing, some in telecommunications. The Human Resources Center also includes a school for 240 physical-

[6]Ibid., pp. 177, 178.

ly disabled youngsters, 60 percent of whom go on to college. Henry Viscardi started the Human Resources Center with an idea and $800 in borrowed money. Twenty-four years later he still has visions for the future. As Chairman of The White House Conference on Handicapped Individuals (1976) his ideas are being heard.[7]

Or, *why not study*

. . . Bernard Bragg, who transformed his world of silence into a new kind of art form — the theatre of the deaf.

or

. . . Harold Russell, who needed no cosmetic help to play the soldier who had lost his hands in the post–World War II film *The Best Years of Our Lives,* and who went on to a lifetime of work for other people with disabilities, including chairmanship of The President's Committee on Employment of the Handicapped.

or

. . . Robert Smithdas

or

. . . Norma Milam

or

. . . The Hliboks

or

. . . Margaret Lester

or

. . . Those Vietnam War veterans who are learning to ski again, but this time on one leg, because they want to feel the grandeur of the sloping earth under them.

or

. . . The participants at The National Wheelchair Games who refuse to give up on their bodies or their right to have fun using them.

[7]P. Bernstein, "The Man Behind Abilities, Inc.," *New York Times,* January 4, 1976, BQLI p. 4. © 1976 by The New York Times Company. Reprinted by permission.

or

. . . The artists whose paintings are painstakingly done with brush in mouth because hands don't work.

Persons with disabilities come in all sizes and shapes, psychologically as well as physically. Some are crippled. Some are like most of us, growing and receding, hurting and healing. Some persons with disabilities are extraordinary. Is this in spite of or because of their disability? Probably sometimes one, sometimes the other, sometimes both or neither.

REFERENCES

BERNSTEIN, P., "The Man Behind Abilities, Inc.," *New York Times,* January 4, 1976, BOLI p. 4.

"Change the Future Now," *The Exceptional Parent,* 5, no. 1 (1975), 5-7.

CHEEVER, R. C., and G. C. CHEEVER, eds., *Laugh with Accent.* Bloomington, Ill.: Accent Special Publications, 1975.

DAVIDSON, A., "Deprived, Exhibited," *New York Times,* January 7, 1976, p. 37.

EPSTEIN, J., *Mermaid on Wheels: The Remarkable Story of Margaret Lester.* New York: Taplinger, 1969. Copyright © 1967 by June Epstein.

FIELDS, S., "Only Human: Conquering the Dark Silence," *The New York Daily News,* January 13, 1976, p. 42.

_____, "Only Human," *The New York Daily News,* July 16, 1975, p. 60.

GREENBERG, J., *In This Sign.* New York: Avon Books, 1970.

HAYNES, R., "Drive With Your Feet," *Accent On Living,* 19, no. 3 (1974), 58-61.

How Does a Blind Person Get Around? New York: American Foundation for the Blind, 1975.

HURWITZ, H. L., *Donald: The Man Who Remains a Boy.* New York: Simon & Schuster (Pocket Books), 1973.

Ideas for Better Living, Twentieth Edition, 1974-75. New York: American Foundation for the Blind.

"Independence?" *The Exceptional Parent,* 4 (1974), 37-42.

"I Was Afraid to Come to College . . . But Then I Met a Guy in a Wheelchair . . .," *Accent On Living,* 20, no. 2 (1975), 42-43.

KLEIN, S. H., "Emergency Attendant Care," *Accent On Living,* 20, no. 2 (1975), 82-86.

Like Other People (16 mm film), distributed by Perennial Education. Northfield, Ill., 1973.

MURRAY, A., "Hope for 'Lincoln's Complaint,' " *New York Times,* February 11, 1973, pp. 71, 88.

" 'New Deal' for Handicapped in Jobs, Housing, Recreation," *U.S. News and World Report,* July 22, 1974, pp. 39-41.

PANZARINO, C., "Denied the Right to Life," *Accent On Living,* 19, no. 3 (1974), 14.

"Person to Person," part III, *The Exceptional Parent,* 3, no. 4 (1973), 45-49.

The President's Committee on Mental Retardation and The President's Committee on Employment of the Handicapped, *These, Too, Must Be Equal: America's Needs in Habilitation and Employment of the Mentally Retarded.* Washington, D.C.: U.S. Government Printing Office, 1974.

SUTHERLAND, P. A., "On the Need of the Severely Handicapped to Feel that They Are Human," *Journal of Rehabilitation,* 34 (1968), 28-30.

WARREN, V. L., "They're All Deaf But, As a Family, They Don't Feel Handicapped," *New York Times,* October 3, 1973, p. 34.

FIVE

Normalization and the Right to a Better Life

A small article recently appeared in the *New York Times* entitled "Outpatient Mental Clinic Draws Protest in Brooklyn." The article mentioned "strong and possibly fatal opposition" from community residents to the proposed clinic.[1] The conclusion and the details were correct, but what was not conveyed was the affect of those community residents.

My daughter had brought the news home to me one Friday in the form of a mimeographed notice she had received at school. There was no identification on the notice indicating where it came from, but its message was clear (See Figure 5-1). It was a call to arms.

[1]G. Lieberman, "Outpatient Mental Clinic Draws Protest in Brooklyn," *New York Times,* March 14, 1976, p. 4BK. © 1976 by The New York Times Company. Reprinted by permission.

On Monday there was a letter from the Parents' Association. The letter gave more details—the clinic would serve patients discharged from state hospitals, as well as people from the community who need help; the board of the Parents' Association had voted against support for this facility (12 to 0 with three abstentions); the board of directors of the community council in

URGENT!   URGENT!

If you CARE!!

Public Hearing Monday March 8, 1976 8 P.M. R. Jr. H. S.

ISSUE

Discussion of Psychiatric Clinic at 15 N. Ave.

BE THERE!!

Numbers Count!!

Figure 5-1

which the school was located had voted against supporting it; the residents of a neighboring area that had originally been selected as the site for the clinic had rejected it. The notice attempted a stance of civic responsibility: "This is as full a picture as I can present based on the information I have received so far. It is my duty to inform you. . . . It is imperative that we turn out . . . to discover for ourselves whether the proposed mental health facility will be detrimental or beneficial to our community. . . ." But the air of impartiality could not be maintained. It alternated with non sequiturs like: "It seems to me that if there are funds available, they could be used to . . . *restore our lost guidance and social work personnel*" [italics added]; and with comments that conveyed a decided attitude: " . . . our community whose quiet residential character has already been seriously compromised by other institutions." Clearly, the Parents' Association was aroused and perceived that something important was at stake.

I went to the meeting with mixed feelings. There were many former patients of state mental institutions already living in the neighborhood. While they didn't seem to present any danger to others, they were at times frightening and bothersome. Some seemed to need help in caring for themselves. Would the new clinic provide them with the sustained help they needed, or would it only stimulate the release of more persons into the community without adequate support? Would the neighborhood, already heavily populated by the aged and increasingly by the poor, tip over into rapid de facto segregation — becoming a community of the needy and helpless — if more former mental patients were released into it?

I arrived about five minutes after eight at the school at which the meeting was to be held. The auditorium was almost completely filled. Someone representing the proposed clinic was speaking about low profiles. There was a loud buzz of conversation in the audience. "What do they think we are, idiots?" I heard a woman behind me say. Then a local politician came on. "I believe the experts know best. . . . I have to trust the professional judgment of the doctors. . . . It's the humane thing to do. . . ." "He's going to support it," the woman beside me stated in alarm. She was wrong. "BUT, I AM TOTALLY OPPOSED!" he finally said. He had been playing his audience, frightening them a bit, raising the level of excitement, all the more to make his rejection of the clinic more striking. There was an outbreak of applause, of whistles and shouts of approval. Then there were questions from the audience, only they weren't questions. They were accusations, epithets, verbal and almost physical fights. There was complete chaos as the chairman banged his gavel and attempted to allow the clinic representatives a chance to answer. They never could. Eventually additional speakers managed to get to the microphone. With the exception of two people from another community where a mental health clinic was already operating, they were all opposed. They cited parking problems, property values, danger to the elderly and to children. "This community is bombarded by social institutions," one speaker said, as if social institutions were some kind of disease. A more sophisticated speaker purported to show that the clinic would not really be good for its clients. It was near a large body of water, for example. What this fact had to do with the quality of treatment was never specified, but lurking in the background was the implied threat that the released mental patients would be irresistibly drawn to either suicide or worse by the presence of a large body of water.

The idea of establishing a mental health clinic in this neighborhood was killed. It did not die a natural death. It died of fear, of hysteria, of false facts. There were questions to be answered that were never asked because no one wanted to give this idea a chance.

What of the people this facility would have served? What happens to them? Perhaps another way will be found, another site, another arrangement. Some people in the community who could have been helped will probably not be. Some former residents of state mental institutions who might have received after-care at the clinic will probably be left to make it on their own.

LEAVE "WELL ENOUGH" ALONE?

Why was the community faced with this choice? Why aren't "crazy" people being kept in institutions? Why do we and our children have to be exposed to a woman who walks through the streets raging at everything and no one; to a young man who stands for hours on the curb of a street staring into space, not moving or talking; to a middle-aged woman who thinks that young boys are bothering her; to a man who dresses in a heavy black overcoat in the middle of summer; to a young woman who won't wear her plastic leg anymore and who walks about the streets on winter days in a short dress that reveals the stump of what was once her other leg? The question troubles me when I think of these people, but I am even more troubled when I think of the alternative most of them have already experienced — the state institution.

"But are the mentally ill, the retarded, and the severely physically handicapped not better off in institutions where they can be taken care of?" you might ask. "Why try to push these people into a world they are not equipped to handle?" For several reasons. First among these is the individual right to liberty.

Mr. Louis Perroni was incarcerated in mental institutions for almost thirteen years because one day he fired a warning shot in the air in a simmering dispute over the property on which his gas station was located. Until that day, Louis Perroni had been a responsible citizen and businessman. He had had no previous problems with the law or with psychiatry. Instead of being tried for his action, he was ordered to undergo a psychiatric examination, which led to his being committed to Matteawan State Hospital (New York State) for the criminally insane. It took the Perroni family six years to obtain a judgment from the state supreme court that he was to be tried or released. Instead, three months later the county court ordered another psychiatric examination.

When Mr. Perroni was first arrested and ordered to undergo psychiatric examination, he cooperated. He talked with the psychiatrists. He explained the reasons for his action. The psychiatrists declared him unfit to stand trial. Seven years later, working with legal counsel this time, he declined to discuss the circumstances surrounding his offense with the psychiatrists on the grounds of self-incrimination. The psychiatrists interpreted his refusal to answer as a sign of " 'lack of cooperativeness' and 'negativism' which added up to 'mental illness' " (Szasz, 1973, p. 106). Louis Perroni was again declared incompetent to stand trial by the examining psychiatrists and was returned to Matteawan State Hospital. Another six years passed before he was finally tried on the original charges, which were then dismissed. In the name of protecting a person who was unable to defend himself in a courtroom, the state deprived Louis Perroni of his freedom for thirteen years because he had fired one shot of a gun into the air.

What happens to people in institutions? Is it better for them there? Are they helped? An interesting experiment took place in a ward at Elgin State Hospital for the mentally ill in Illinois. During a three-day holiday weekend, twenty-nine volunteer members of the staff took on the role of patients, and were exposed to the standard patient treatment in that institution. They were "admitted" to the hospital, showered, body checked, given institution clothing, and taken to the locked ward where they were introduced to the staff but not vice versa. The "patients" had to request the staff to light their cigarettes (patients are not allowed to use matches), unlock doors for them, get them coffee. The staff discussed supposedly private patient problems among themselves in the presence of the "patients" but without including them in the discussion. The "patients" used the unlocked toilets, were not allowed to use the dormitory during daytime, and lined up with actual mental patients in the cafeteria for meals.

Something started to happen. Changes took place. The behavior of staff members quickly began to resemble that of actual mental patients. There was incessant pacing back and forth, and lack of verbal communication. Windows were broken and there were several escape attempts. Some "patients" wept uncontrollably. There was stealing, depression, hostility, and complaints about "dehumanizing" conditions (Orlando, 1973).

We put people in mental institutions because their deviant behavior leads us to believe that they cannot care for themselves, or are a danger to others. We put them in institutions which exacerbate the very behaviors that originally caused the institutionalization.

In 1976 the film *One Flew Over the Cuckoo's Nest* swept the Academy Awards, winning in the categories of best screenplay, best director, best actor, best actress, best picture. It was a film that affected people strongly. This movie was about a man who discovered that the normal procedures of a mental institution, its ethos, its essence, was fatal to being human.

McMurphy looks at me awhile, then turns back to Harding. "Man, I tell you, how come you stand for it? What about this democratic-ward manure that the doctor was giving me? Why don't you take a vote?"

Harding smiles at him and takes another slow drag on his cigarette. "Vote what, my friend? Vote that the nurse may not ask any more questions in Group Meeting? Vote that she shall not *look* at us in a certain way? You tell me, Mr. McMurphy, what do we vote on?"

"Hell, I don't care. Vote on anything. Don't you see you have to do something to show you still got some guts? Don't you see you can't let her take over completely? . . . I never saw a scareder-looking bunch in my life than you guys."

"Not me!" Cheswick says.

"Maybe not you, buddy, but the rest are even scared to open up and *laugh*. You know, that's the first thing that got me about this place, that there wasn't anybody laughing. I haven't heard a real laugh since I came through that door."[2]

This film was a fictional piece of work, not a documentary, but the story it told is real enough.

When I first got there, they showed me into the day room. I sat there for an hour and no one said anything to me. I was too scared to talk to anyone else. Then they came and told me to come and take some medication. They doped me up pretty heavily. I think it was 250 milograms of Thorazine and some Seconal, which is quite a heavy dose of medication. Everyone was overdrugged. They didn't even bother to ask me if I was allergic to anything. . . .

There weren't any seats on the johns. You sat on the bare porcelain. Sometimes there was toilet paper, and sometimes not. If there wasn't any toilet paper, you tried to talk an attendant into letting you go to the place where they kept it. If he didn't feel like doing it, he didn't. It was totally up to him. The whole thing was so humiliating.

While I was there, I felt less than human, but you could never say that. The one thing that you don't do there is to tell people the way you feel. If you complain about something, you're through. They say you're fighting the system. They tell you you're not cooperative. The worst thing you can be is uncooperative. That means doing anything they don't want. It goes on your record. Can you imagine the big book in the office—it's like God sitting up there scaring you. That is exactly the way a patient feels in the hospital. Everything that you do gets put on that chart. They watch every move that you make. You try to make your record look good. Forget about being human—you can't. (Bogdan, 1974, pp. 186, 187–88, 193)

Institutions are designed for persons who are not fully human. The disabled—the disturbed, the retarded, the multiply handicapped—have been conceptualized as subhuman throughout many ages. They were, and are still, referred to as

[2]From *One Flew Over The Cuckoo's Nest,* by Ken Kesey, p. 65. Copyright © 1962 by Ken Kesey. Reprinted by permission of the Viking Press and Calder and Boyars Ltd., London.

vegetables or animals. When people are conceived of as less than human, all kinds of treatment that would not be tolerated for humans is allowed. Lack of choice, lack of toilet seats, lack of information, lack of consultation—what about it? Do you consult with your pet dog? Do you inform him of the vet's treatment plans when he is ill? Do you ask him if he wants to be walked? Why bother with these things if you are dealing with subhuman beings?

> Noted physicians, researchers, professors and parents, all serving as witnesses, told stories of bruised and beaten children, maggot-infested wounds, assembly-line bathing, inadequate medical care, cruel and inappropriate use of restraints, and inadequate clothing . . . at the Willowbrook institution. (President's Committee on Mental Retardation, 1975, p. 88)

Expressions of this view of the disabled as subhuman can be found throughout the designs and programs of institutions (Wolfensberger, 1975). Animals are primitive and uncontrolled: Lock the doors of the living units and the sub-areas within them. Vegetables are not capable of making meaningful choices: Make light switches inaccessible to residents, make showers controllable only by staff, give everyone the same clothes. Animals must be controlled: Give high dosages of drugs; watch them constantly, keep them away from people. Vegetables cannot be expected to learn or develop appreciably: Don't bother with educational or vocational programs. Animals have few rights: There is no need to make provisions for personal property, or to arrange for payment for work performed. Animals and vegetables have no sensibilities, no awareness or shame: There is no need for privacy, for doors on toilets or showers.

The problem with this stance is that only a tiny fraction of those people we put away from us and hide in institutions cannot, or need to be unable, to understand, to feel, to choose.

> To me there never was a State School. The words State School sound like a place with vocational training or you get some sort of

education. That's just not the way Empire State School is. They have taken millions of dollars and spent them and never rehabilitated who they were supposed to. If you looked at individuals and see what they said they were supposed to do for that person and then what they actually did, you would find that many of them were actually hurt—not helped. I don't like the word vegetable, but in my own case I could see that if I had been placed on the low grade ward I might have slipped to that. I began feeling myself slip. They could have made me a vegetable. If I would have let that place get to me and depress me I would still have been there today. Actually, it was one man that saved me. . . . I had just arrived at the place. I was trying to understand what was happening. I was confused. . . . There was this supervisor, a woman. She came on to the ward and looked right at me and said: "I have him scheduled for P-8." An older attendant was there. He looked over at me and said, "He's too bright for that ward. I think we'll keep him." . . .

Of course I didn't know what P-8 was then, but I found out. I visited up there a few times on work detail. That man saved my life. (Bogdan and Taylor, 1976, p. 49)

There is something fundamentally wrong with our institutions for the disabled, with their basic conceptualization. They are not designed to help people grow.

Kenneth Donaldson was 63 years old when he was released from Florida State Hospital, where he had spent almost fifteen years. After being civilly committed, and then diagnosed as a paranoid schizophrenic, Mr. Donaldson had made numerous unsuccessful attempts to gain his own release. There was no evidence that he had ever been dangerous to himself or others. During his almost fifteen years of hospitalization he received no treatment, and for substantial periods of time he was simply kept in a large room that housed sixty patients, many of them criminally committed. The hospital superintendent, psychiatrist J. B. O'Connor, refused to release Mr. Donaldson even after a halfway house and a longtime friend offered to assume responsibility for his welfare.

He and McMurphy had got to talking about the difference between hospital and jail, and McMurphy was saying how much better the hospital was. The lifeguard wasn't so sure. I heard him tell McMurphy that, for one thing, being committed ain't like being sentenced. "You're sentenced in a jail, and you got a date ahead of you when you *know* you're gonna be turned loose," he said.

McMurphy stopped splashing around like he had been. He swam slowly to the edge of the pool and held there, looking up at the lifeguard. "And if you're committed?" he asked after a pause.

The lifeguard raised his shoulders in a muscle-bound shrug. . . .[3]

In June 1975 the U.S. Supreme Court ruled unanimously that nondangerous persons who were capable of surviving safely by themselves or with the help of responsible, willing friends or relatives, could not be confined by the state in institutions providing only custodial care (*"O'Connor* v. *Donaldson*: An Analysis," 1975). At issue was the constitutional right to liberty. We cannot exile people because we find their presence upsetting, or because we believe that they would be better off in a custodial institution, ruled the Supreme Court.

> May the state fence in the harmlessly mentally ill solely to save its citizens from exposure to those whose ways are different? One might as well ask if the state, to avoid public unease, could incarcerate all who are physically unattractive or socially eccentric. Mere public intolerance or animosity cannot constitutionally justify the deprivation of . . . physical liberty. . . .
>
> The mere presence of mental illness does not disqualify a person from preferring his home to the comforts of an institution. (President's Committee on Mental Retardation, 1975, pp. 1, 2)

The mentally handicapped are citizens with full constitutional rights like the rest of us. The Supreme Court ruling made this official public policy.

[3]From *One Flew Over the Cuckoo's Nest,* by Ken Kesey, p. 147. Copyright © 1962 by Ken Kesey. Reprinted by permission of the Viking Press and Calder and Boyars Ltd., London.

What of those tens of thousands who are still in institutions and will remain there? To what are they entitled? What prospects are there for them? The Supreme Court evaded this issue in the *O'Connor* v. *Donaldson* decision, but the state courts have not done so. On March 12, 1971, a formal decree was issued in Alabama, in the case of *Wyatt* v. *Hardin,* which held that patients involuntarily committed to a state institution because of mental illness had a constitutional right to treatment that would offer a realistic opportunity for improvement. The judge gave the State Commissioner of Mental Health six months to institute such treatment. At the end of the six-month period the court ruled that minimum treatment standards had not been promulgated. With the aid of representatives of the Ameican Psychological Association, the American Orthopsychiatric Association, the American Civil Liberties Union, and the American Association on Mental Deficiency, the court issued an order setting standards for minimum treatment. In November 1974 the United States Court of Appeals for the Fifth Circuit, responding to an appeal by the Alabama Mental Health Board and then Governor George Wallace, unanimously upheld the decision of the state court that the Constitution guarantees civilly committed persons in state mental institutions a right to treatment.

> The doctor had finished his spiel, and the nurse had opened right up with, "Now. Who will start? Let out those old secrets." And she'd put all the Acutes in a trance by sitting there in silence for twenty minutes after the question, quiet as an electric alarm about to go off, waiting for somebody to start telling something about themselves. Her eyes swept back and forth over them as steady as a turning beacon. The day room was clamped silent for twenty long minutes, with all of the patients stunned where they sat. When twenty minutes had passed, she looked at her watch and said, "Am I to take it that there's not a man among you that has committed some act that he has never admitted?" She reached in the basket for the log book. "Must we go over past history?"

That triggered something, some acoustic device in the walls, rigged to turn on at just the sound of those words coming from her mouth. The Acutes stiffened. Their mouths opened in unison. Her sweeping eyes stopped on the first man along the wall.

His mouth worked. "I robbed a cash register in a service station."

She moved to the next man.

"I tried to take my little sister to bed."

Her eyes clicked to the next man; each one jumped like a shooting-gallery target.

"I — one time — wanted to take my brother to bed."

"I killed my cat when I was six. Oh, God forgive me, I stoned her to death and said my neighbor did it."

"I lied about trying. I did take my sister!"

"So did I! So did I!"

"And me! And *me!*"

It was better than she'd dreamed. They were all shouting to outdo one another, going further and further, no way of stopping, telling things that wouldn't ever let them look one another in the eye again. The nurse nodding at each confession and saying Yes, yes, yes.

Then old Pete was on his feet. "I'm *tired!*" was what he shouted, a strong, angry copper tone to his voice that no one had ever heard before.

Everyone hushed. They were somehow ashamed. It was as if he had suddenly said something that was real and true and important and it had put all their childish hollering to shame. The Big Nurse was furious. She swiveled and glared at him, the smile dripping over her chin; she'd just had it going so good.[4]

The Court of Appeals decision in the case of *Wyatt* v. *Hardin* has served as a model for legal and administrative stan-

---

[4]From *One Flew Over the Cuckoo's Nest*, by Ken Kesey, pp. 49-50. Copyright © 1962 by Ken Kesey. Reprinted by permission of The Viking Press and Calder and Boyars Ltd., London.

dards across the country. What changes did this decision, and the minimum treatment standards set up in it, make to the residents of state institutions in Alabama? More staff was hired, safety hazards were corrected, sanitation was improved. The state budget for mental institutions increased fourfold in six years, in spite of the fact that the in-patient population was cut in half. But the most critical aspect of the court decision, the right to individualized treatment, appeared not to have been fulfilled ("Wyatt Victory 'Tarnished'?," 1975).

We have had exposés of institutions by Geraldo Rivera and Robert Kennedy and by many dedicated professionals and by advocate groups. We now have legal decrees at the state level, the regional level, and the national level which define minimal constitutional standards. They have succeeded in correcting only some of the most blatant abuses, and even these slowly.

> An Assembly study group says that despite repeated reports of the poor care and treatment of patients at state mental institutions . . . treatment plans at such facilities are totally inadequate or nonexistent. . . .
>
> Despite substantial increases in funding and staff, coupled with an increase in public awareness which has prompted a number of reforms, our mentally disabled are still warehoused. (*New York Post,* October 8, 1975, p. 51)

Conceptualizations and habits change slowly. Institution workers who have been functioning primarily as caretakers cannot suddenly become therapeutic or education assistants. People who perceive themselves as managers of vegetables cannot overnight conceive of the mentally ill or retarded as capable of development. People who defined their roles as controlling animals cannot easily shift to roles as trainers of independence and decision-making abilities. Psychiatrists who previously functioned with almost no restrictions governing their professional decisions won't find it easy to be held to a standard of informed consent. Between April 1972 and May 1974 several patients at

Bryce Hospital, the original institution in question in the *Wyatt v. Hardin* case, were given electro-convulsive therapy without their consent, in direct violation of one of the standards set by the court decree. The electro-convulsive therapy was administered in accordance with a hospital policy directive.

A switch snaps the clasps on his wrists, ankles, clamping him into the shadow. A hand takes off his wristwatch, won it from Scanlon, drops it near the panel, it springs open, cogs and wheels and the long dribbling spiral of spring jumping against the side of the panel and sticking fast.

He don't look a bit scared. He keeps grinning at me.

They put the graphite salve on his temples. "What is it?" he says. "Conductant," the technician says.

"Anointest my head with conductant. Do I get a crown of thorns?"

They smear it on. He's singing to them, makes their hands shake.

" 'Get Wildroot Cream Oil, Cholly. . . .' "

Put on those things like headphones, crown of silver thorns over the graphite at his temples. They try to hush his singing with a piece of rubber hose for him to bite on.

" 'Mage with thoothing lan-o-lin.' "

Twist some dials, and the machine trembles, two robot arms pick up soldering irons and hunch down on him. He gives me the wink and speaks to me, muffled, tells me something, says something to me around that rubber hose just as those irons get close enough to the silver on his temples — light arcs across, stiffens him, bridges him up off the table till nothing is down but his wrists and ankles and out around that crimped black rubber hose a sound like *hooeee!* and he's frosted over completely with sparks. . . .

They roll him out on a Gurney, still jerking, face frosted white. Corrosion. Battery acid.[5]

[5]From *One Flew Over the Cuckoo's Nest*, by Ken Kesey, pp. 237–38. Copyright © 1962 by Ken Kesey. Reprinted by permission of The Viking Press and Calder and Boyars Ltd., London.

ALTERNATIVES

A movement, a groundswell, is sweeping our country. It grew from many sources — from muckrakers with their exposés; from groups of parents unwilling to let their children live forever in warehouses; from professionals who were ashamed of what their profession was doing to the disabled. The name that is sometimes given to this movement is "normalization." Normalization is defined as "utilization of means as culturally normative as possible to establish and/or maintain personal behaviors and characteristics which are as culturally normative as possible" (Wolfensberger, 1972, p. 28).

The goal for every disabled person is life in the least restrictive setting possible. People who can be helped to function in group homes or hotels should not be kept in institutions. People who can function in their own homes with supportive help should be given this supportive help rather than be kept in group homes. The means — the treatment, training, education — used with disabled persons should be directed toward fostering the maximum possible independent functioning. The means used should be a sequentially designed series of steps toward this goal.

" 'Can you help me get out?' The request came unexpectedly from a man raking up leaves on the institution grounds" (President's Committee on Mental Retardation, 1974, p. 19). He was 70 years old, but he had heard about the program of training for community living and he wanted to be part of it. Now he is living in a group home, working in a sheltered workshop, and having the time of his life.

" 'This is really living,' he says, as he draws up a chair for a checkers game with the other men after dinner" (Ibid., p. 19).

Is there any role for state institutions or hospitals? Yes, but probably not as we know them today:

— There is now and will be in the future a need for residential centers where persons can come for temporary periods of recuperation, support and guidance, when their ability to live in society is faltering.

— There is now and will be in the future a need for short-term residential treatment centers where the mentally retarded can come to obtain clearly specified training designed to enable them to live at home or function in a community setting. A child may stay for two or three or four months while he is trained to feed himself and take care of his toileting needs independently. At a later time he may return for another short period for additional specified training.

— There is now and will be in the future a need for residential centers that will provide respite care periodically for families of the severely disabled. State hospitals can be designed to operate such programs of periodic temporary care.

— There is now and will be in the future a need for long-term caring facilities for the small number of severely and profoundly impaired individuals who, even with the best of treatment, remain a serious danger to themselves or others. For them, institutions must become homes, redesigned to allow for the greatest possible comfort, growth, and choice.

The number of individuals for whom long-term institutional care is needed is considerably smaller than the number of individuals in institutions today, even though these institutions have discharged thousands of patients in great haste recently.

In 1970 the president defined a goal of enabling one-third of the more than 200,000 retarded persons in institutions to return to useful lives in their communities. Many states have moved close to this goal. How useful or successful the lives of these people are is another question, with a wide range of answers. For some the answers are happy ones.

When he was six, Johnny was still in diapers. He was able to say four or five words, and could barely walk. All day long for six years he had stared at the blank walls of a crowded ward . . . where he had been brought shortly after he was born.

Severely retarded, he faced only the prospect of eventually moving into another ward. . . .

But one day Johnny was taken out of the back ward and into a hostel in Omaha where five other severely retarded youngsters were living.

Johnny now is a lively little boy who goes to special education classes; he talks and sings, goes down the sliding board, dresses himself and, of course, is toilet trained. Five days a week he, along with the others of the "family," are bused to their special classes, physical therapy and recreation programs.

Perhaps more important, he is being introduced to normal living, in a real home, on a real street, and living with a real couple who are taking on the role of parents. (President's Committee on Mental Retardation, 1973, pp. 42-43)

Henry came out of Beatrice [State School] when he was 46, after 38 years on the back wards. His records said he was totally incapable of functioning outside." Henry moved into a hostel in Omaha and was given five months of intensive vocational and social training. He has not missed one day of work nor been late once for his job as a dishwasher in an Omaha restaurant. (President's Committee on Mental Retardation, 1973, pp. 42-43)

When institution residents are released into the community, they can go to hostels, halfway houses, group homes, nursing homes, foster homes, boarding homes, their own family homes, their own apartments, furnished hotel rooms. They can be programmed into sheltered workshops, day-care training programs or jobs; or, they can be left to devise their own ways of filling their days. They can be given regular follow-up care and guidance, or they can be forgotten.

Mansfield Training School in Connecticut wants to have its cake and eat it too. It has a "clothing store" where the residents choose their own clothes:

"Why dole clothes out, when they can come in and choose what they like? . . . Besides, they'll have to get used to buying clothes when they leave." (President's Committee on Mental Retardation, 1973, p. 37)

The snack bar is staffed by residents, patronized by staff and residents alike.

> "We got a little flack . . . when we decided to open the staff's snack bar up to the whole place. So we started with the 'high level' residents only, one day a week. Eventually, they were all coming, any time they wanted to. Nobody gives it a second thought any more." . . .
>
> Whenever possible, the children go to local public schools. . . .
>
> Many of the retarded adults hold jobs in neighboring industries. . . .
>
> A resident in his late 50s proudly shows off his room, furnished homestyle, complete with color TV. He paid for the television and most of the furniture with money he has earned working at Goodwill Industries. . . .
>
> A group of teenagers in the new Kennedy Cottage . . . discuss their future with excitement as they prepare their own dinner. . . .
>
> "We do anything we can to close the gap between the community and our residents. . . . Look, it may seem like a country club, but it's still an institution. And an institution is an institution. . . . The idea is to get as many as we can into real life, or as close to it as possible." . . .
>
> Throughout the region, there are former Mansfield residents living in group homes, some in boarding homes, a few living independently. Mansfield has leased the homes, and Mansfield staff remains available when needed, in addition to the house parents who are there at all times. (Ibid., pp. 37–40)

It can be done right. We know the way. Unfortunately, the right way is only occasionally the way we do it. Few social reversals have occurred as quickly as the dramatic swing from institutional care to community placement. Inevitably, dislocations, disruptions, mistakes have occurred. There have been dramatic successes and "carefully screened-over failures" (Crissey, 1975, p. 806).

State institutions for the mentally ill are also releasing thousands of patients. While some self-help groups, halfway houses, and follow-up treatment programs exist, on the whole the picture for these people is bleak.

> State mental hospitals are releasing thousands of long-term mental patients and placing them in private, profit-making proprietary homes where they are virtually abandoned and are forced to live on allowances of less than 50 cents a day. . . .
>
> The patients, who become free citizens on their release, wander the streets of Queens and Brooklyn, nearly all heavily medicated and dressed in the tattered hand-me-downs of strangers. Much of their time is spent panhandling for a little extra spending money. (Browne, 1975, p. B1)

In the fall of 1975 all Medicaid and Medicare funds to Pilgrim Psychiatric Center, a mental hospital operated by New York State, were cut off. Pilgrim had lost its accreditation because of stiffening standards involving patient-staff ratios, rights to treatment, and rights to privacy. Ordinarily, the hospital would have been given extensions to the cutoff in funds while it endeavored to regain accreditation. This time there were no extensions because an advocate group took an active role in blocking the payments. The advocate group, Federation of Parents' Organizations for the New York State Mental Institutions, was attempting to obtain guarantees that the 1,500 residents to be released from Pilgrim State Hospital would not just be dumped into the community without adequate provision for their care. When the state would not commit itself to a document embodying these guarantees, the parents' group acted to block federal funds (Yuncker, 1975, p. 13).

In the one-year period ending March 31, 1975 approximately 16,500 persons whose official residence was New York City were released from state institutions. Undoubtedly, many of these persons could be said to have been dumped.

There is a woman who roams the neighborhood in which I live. Sometimes she is a gentle, grandmotherly type, with her white hair and shy, friendly smile. At other times she shrieks and rages, cursing her lot, accusing all around her. I hear her late at night when I am in my apartment on the fifteenth floor. Sometimes I pass her on the street when I am walking my dog or going out with my daughter. My daughter and my dog are terrified of her when she is in one of her states. She used to frighten me too.

And I often pass the grime-covered, late 30ish man whom I used to know when we were both adolescents. He walks about the streets talking to himself, oblivious to anyone else, to how he looks, how he smells. He was released recently from a state mental institution in the great rush to comply with the right to liberty decision; now he has the liberty to walk the streets in oblivion. Where is his halfway house, his sheltered workshop, his follow-up, his plan, training, right to treatment?

ANOTHER PERSPECTIVE

On September 3, 1967 motorists in Sweden switched over to driving on the right side of the road, after four years of preparation for this change. The extensive planning worked. The changeover, which involved redesign of vehicles, streets, highways, traffic signs, etc., was accomplished with a minimum of disruption and damage. A major part of the planning had involved preparations for the handicapped.

"But why so much special effort?" I asked Mr. Skjöld, and later Mr. Arnor. "Surely the blind do not drive in Sweden—and probably there are not so many crippled or mentally retarded drivers that they required all this special attention?"

The answer illuminated the thinking of the Swedes. "No, the blind, the crippled and the mentally retarded do not drive—but they are affected by driving. They are passengers . . . they are pedestrians . . . they are part of the world around the driver . . . they are part of our society. And so we had to make sure that their safety too was insured." (Lippman, 1972, p. 15)

The problem of preparing the mentally retarded for this change in traffic patterns was the most difficult, since it required time and repetition, and since the retarded might apply their new learning too soon if they were trained in advance. Instead, a massive effort was mounted to reach parents of the retarded. There were meetings in every county of Sweden. A special illustrated pamphlet of instructions was distributed through schools, day centers, and other facilities for retarded persons. Special material for retarded children and adolescents was shown on popular television programs. There were special radio and television programs for parents of the retarded during the week preceding the traffic change. There were also spot announcements and television programs to inform the general public about the problems of the handicapped in adjusting to the coming change. The Swedish attitude toward handicapped persons was reflected in the care that was devoted to the handicapped during its period of national societal change.

In 1970 a three-day conference took place in Malmo, Sweden in which fifty mentally retarded persons came together to discuss problems of residential living, vocational training, work, and leisure-time activities. The fifty participants were delegates representing the retarded in twenty-four of Sweden's twenty-five counties. They were mildly and moderately retarded young adults who had experienced special classes, schools, hostels, institutions, and sheltered workshops, and who had served on councils of the retarded in these facilities. That a national conference *of* (not for) the retarded would be called is still a source of amazement to most of us. Not so to the Danes or Swedes who recommended in 1969 and 1970 the establishment of councils for the retarded in all facilities for the retarded. That the fifty retarded delegates formulated conclusions and recommendations that could serve as one important source for future policy considerations is even more amazing to us. Let us look at some of these conclusions.

> We wish to have an apartment of our own and not be coddled by personnel; therefore we want courses in cooking, budgeting, etc. . . .
>
> We want the right to move together with members of the opposite sex when we feel ready for it, and we also want the right to marry when we ourselves find the time is right.
>
> We want to have more personal freedom, and not as it is now in certain institutions and boarding homes where you have to ask for permission to shop for fruit, newspaper, tobacco, etc.
>
> We want the right to invite other youngsters to our hostels. . . .
>
> When we are living in institutions, we want social training so as to be able to move out into society and manage on our own. . . .
>
> We demand that our capacity for work should not be underestimated.
>
> We want that when we are working in the open job market, our fellow workers should be informed about our handicap. . . .
>
> We think that we should be present when our situation is discussed by doctors, teachers, welfare workers, foremen, etc. Now, it feels as if they talk behind our backs.
>
> We demand to have more information about our handicap, and the possibilities we have of entering the open market. (Wolfensberger, 1972, pp. 190–192)

These retarded adults were asking to be treated with honesty; to be included in decisions about their own futures; to be recognized as being capable of growth and responsibility.

HOW NOW?

Where does this leave us? We have institutions that are warehouses and institutions that are not so bad. We have people in institutions who will need total care for the rest of their lives, but we have people in institutions who can be taught to function, and others who should never have been there in the first place. We have institutions discharging residents to better places and better programs, but we have institutions discharging residents to no programs and any kind of place. We have hostels and group homes that are working, but we have other halfway placements where no one is even trying. We have communities that are pitching in to make a go of this societal shift, and we have communities that are frightened of it and fight it. We have people learning to work and live on their own, but we also have people wandering about the streets with no one to help.

Next door to where I live is a hotel that has seen better days. Some people call it a "welfare" hotel. Its once blue-green pool is never filled any more. Its once-showy lobby is becoming shabby. Its tourist visitors from abroad have been long gone, and so too its summer vacation guests. There are new kinds of residents here now. Some are families with young children staying temporarily until the city's social service department can find them apartments. Some are the elderly, who mark their time by the day their social security check arrives. Then there are others, old and young. Like the elderly they seem to have few friends or relatives. Most of the day they stand about alone, doing nothing in particular. This is their alternative.

I never know what to do when I see a "shopping bag lady" with the sum total of her possessions packed in bags she carries at all times, sleeping in layers of clothes in subways or hallways or parks. I am often tempted to call the Welfare Department or even the police to ask whether there isn't a place somewhere for such a person, but I already know the answer. We have jails and we have warehouses. Our courts are guarding us against unconstitutional detention and involuntary commitment. But there are cracks wide enough for tens or even hundreds of thousands to fall through. These are people who have no one and no place to belong. They need help, but they need a hand that won't rob them of their most important possession—the right to decide for themselves.

Last year Yolanda came out of the State School where she had been since she was two years old. She had stayed there for 16 years. . . .

Yolanda originally had requested the business course at the occupational center where she was trained for employment but, because of her past experience with failure, *the staff preferred* [italics mine] to start her in something less stressful. So she was prepared for food services instead. . . .

Her first attempt to hold a food services job and live in a group home failed, and she had to return to the institution.

The second venture into the world has succeeded. . . .

Through her own initiative, she has parlayed a job from messenger to "office assistant," maintaining office supplies, and opening and closing the office each day, since she is on the job earlier and later than anyone else.

In a project she calls her "insurance for the future," she is teaching herself to type. (President's Committee on Mental Retardation, 1974, p. 8)

REFERENCES

BOGDAN, R., *Being Different: The Autobiography of Jane Fry.* New York: Wiley, 1974.

BOGDAN, R., and S. TAYLOR, "The Judged, Not the Judges," *American Psychologist,* 31 (1976), 47–52.

BROWNE, A., "Money Woe Haunts Ex-Mental Patients," *New York Sunday News,* August 24, 1975.

CRISSEY, M. S., "Mental Retardation: Past, Present, and Future," *American Psychologist,* 30 (1975), 800–808.

KESEY, K., *One Flew Over the Cuckoo's Nest.* New York: New American Library, 1962.

LIEBERMAN, G., "Outpatient Mental Clinic Draws Protest in Brooklyn," *New York Times,* March 14, 1976, p. 4 BK.

"O'CONNOR v. DONALDSON: An Analysis," *Amicus,* 1, no. 1 (1975), 10–11.

ORLANDO, N. J., "The Mock Ward: A Study in Simulation," *Behavior Disorders: Perspectives and Trends,* ed. O. Milton and R. G. Wahler, pp. 162–70. Philadelphia: Lippincott, 1973.

President's Committee on Mental Retardation, *Mental Retardation and the Law: A Report on Status of Current Court Cases.* Washington, D.C.: Department of Health, Education and Welfare Publication No. (OHD) 76-21012, 1975.

President's Committee on Mental Retardation, *MR 72: Islands of Excellence.* Washington, D.C.: Department of Health, Education and Welfare Publication No. (05) 73-7, 1973.

President's Committee on Mental Retardation, *MR 73: The Goal Is Freedom.* Washington, D.C.: Department of Health, Education and Welfare Publication No. (OHD) 74-21001, 1974.

SZASZ, T. S., "Psychiatric Justice: The Case of Mr. Louis Perroni," in *Behavior Disorders: Perspectives and Trends,* ed. O. Milton and R. G. Wahler, pp. 64–107. Philadelphia: Lippincott, 1973.

WOLFENSBERGER, W., *Normalization: The Principle of Normalization in Human Services.* Toronto: National Institute on Mental Retardation, 1972.

⸻, *The Origin and Nature of Our Institutional Models.* Syracuse: Human Policy Press, 1975.

"Wyatt Victory 'Tarnished'?", *APA Monitor,* 6 (September/October 1975).

YUNCKER, B., "The Mental Hospital $$ Row," *New York Post,* November 5, 1975, p. 13.

SIX

Education for All

Yesterday twenty graduate students spent 2½ hours with me studying methods of toilet training. We drew charts and graphs, talked about pinpointing and scheduling and reinforcing. We did a step-by-step analysis of the process of independent toileting. Later I was conducting a discussion at a conference. The participants were administrators of educational programs for severely disabled children. A few university professors were also present. The discussion came around to toilet training. One of the professors asked me to elucidate my thinking about the role of the special education teacher as toilet trainer. Suddenly the whole situation seemed very funny to me. Here I was, Ph.D. in psychology with a long history of academic honors and awards, giving a treatise on toilet training, the bane of existence for countless thousands of young mothers, the epitome of housewifely drudgery! After controlling my momentary impulse to erupt with laughter, I replied that I would like to think of toilet training as a function rather than a role; much as I recognized its importance in education, I wouldn't feel quite right about thinking of myself as "a toilet trainer."

But this was a very serious topic with major implications for education. The fact that toilet training is now a subject of graduate courses and conferences is a reflection of a revolution that has taken place recently in the field of special education. Just a few years ago independent toilet training was the sine qua non for admission into almost any public or private school program for the handicapped, no matter how young the children involved. A more effective tool for screening out the severely disabled could hardly have been devised! In 1965 a 20-year-old black man from a poor area of Chicago was accused of the murder of a prostitute. The unusual aspect of this case was that the man had no means of communication. He could not speak, write, read, or use sign language. He had been deaf since birth or early infancy and his entire education had begun and ended at age 2½. At 2½ years of age this man had been admitted to a school for the deaf, from which he was quickly "expelled." The problem: he was inadequately toilet trained (Tidyman, 1975).

Parents of "normal" babies generally accept as their responsibility the task of helping their children learn the basics of language, and elementary self-help skills—toileting, feeding, and dressing—before they enter school. When a child's mind and body are intact this doesn't usually present any serious problems. Most children are eager for independence. A 15-month-old may grab the spoon from his mother and insist on feeding himself. Not too much later he will have developed the necessary skills to do so. A 2-year-old may insist on dressing himself, and although his mother may be appalled at his appearance at first, in a relatively short period of time he will be able to manage the basics of dressing. By age 3 most children can manage, most of the time, to get to the toilet to perform the functions we expect them to perform there. When serious problems arise in this process, we sometimes find a parent or parents who are ill-equipped to deal with young children. Often, we will find a handicapped child. These same developmental accomplishments which are so easy for an intact child may, in fact, be the basic curriculum of a special education program for a long time. When schools insisted upon toilet training as the admission ticket for kindergarten they hardly taxed the parents of normal children; but when schools insisted upon toilet training as an admission ticket into special education programs, they placed an enormous burden upon the parents of many of these children, and they deprived thousands of children of their right to an education.

THE RIGHT TO EDUCATION

In the fall of 1975 a landmark bill was passed by the Congress of the United States and signed into law by the president. Public Law 94-142, The Education of All Handicapped Children Act of 1975, can be thought of as the "Bill of Rights for Handicapped Children" (Abeson and Ballard, 1976, p. 83). It was the culmination of years of change in public policy toward disabled children; change from widespread exclusion and isolation to the recognition of full educational rights; a change stimulated and prodded along by numerous, favorable court decisions in the period from 1971 to 1974. The Education of All Handicapped Children Act affirms the absolute, constitutional right of every child to an education: *Every* child has a right to an education; education is essential for every child; every (exceptional) child is capable of benefiting from education. The purpose and design of this law was to terminate the exclusion of handicapped children from the public education system (Abeson and Ballard, 1976).

The last refuges and subterfuges for excluding the disabled were stripped away. No more "postponements" of admission until the child attains a particular mental age — a mental age which he may never attain without instruction! No more waiting lists for educational services. No more medical discharges that lead to nothing. No more tuition grants to private schools that parents can't afford to use because the private schools charge much more. No more home instruction for endless years for children who need to learn to live with others. Free public education for every child without exception.

Public policy has changed. By the beginning of the new school year in 1978 each state that wishes to partake of the financial benefits of P.L. 94-142 must provide a free public education for all handicapped children aged 3* to 18. By 1980 such education must be available to all handicapped individuals up to 21* years of age. The financial incentives are enticing. The federal government will pay a gradually escalating percentage of the cost of educating each handicapped child, until such reimbursement reaches the level of 40 percent of the national average expenditure per public school pupil. The total amount of federal fiscal commitment this would involve would be over $3 billion per year by 1982. And this is to be a permanent commitment, not one that needs to be renewed yearly, as in the past.

Public policy has changed, but this change has created an enormous task for public education. How does one go about educating a child whose IQ is 25, and who has not even been considered trainable in the past? How does one go about educating a child who does not communicate in any way? How does one go about educating a child who cannot sit or hold his head up? Public education had never faced such a challenge before.

TEACHING THE SEVERELY HANDICAPPED

Sam was going to have to leave the residential treatment center where he had been "on trial" for six months. He hadn't made it. There was no place left to try. Custodial placement loomed

*If not incompatible with state law.

ahead. I was Sam's teacher and I hadn't given up on him. I asked for more time. "What has he learned in six months?" the psychiatrist asked. "We are wasting a valuable place that another child can benefit from." "But he is learning," I replied, with somewhat more assurance that I felt. "He is trying to communicate with me. He is producing all kinds of sounds and inflections while looking directly at me. He is even making a sound almost like 'ma ma.' He *is* learning."

Sam was learning, but his achievements were difficult to appreciate because Sam was almost 7 years old, while his progress represented development appropriate for a child of 9 to 12 months. I thought back to when Sam first came to my class. He had been afraid. He crept under a table and covered his head with a piece of newspaper, as if to communicate that this world and its demands were too much for him. Day after day he would go there and lay unmoving until I half-coaxed, half-pulled him out. Then he would bury his head in my body or try to hide under my dress. Sometimes things would happen to him that he couldn't understand or cope with. He tripped over an untied shoelace and beat his head against the floor. Little children, 2- or 3-year-olds, often ascribe life to inanimate objects. Did Sam think the floor had tripped him? Was he venting his anger at the floor? One day he smashed the window on the classroom door with his head. Why? Did he not understand that he could be hurt if he did this? Did he want to hurt himself? Was he oblivious to pain, as some severely retarded or autistic children appear to be at times?

It had been a very slow process to wean this child away from his womblike withdrawal and his self-punishment. It had been a process of feeding and tolerating and giving and protecting. He felt safe with me now. We played games together. He had begun to imitate. He had begun to laugh. Now I would be unable to do any more.

Sam might never have learned to speak in sentences, or read or write, but he could learn. In 1962, unhappily, this level of learning was not valued enough to be considered worth continuing. I have thought of Sam many times in the years since then. I have thought of him hiding again and banging his head, the laughter long since extinguished. It is for children like Sam that P.L. 94-142 can mean a real chance at laughter.

In times past there was a kind of mocking association between teachers of the handicapped and their pupils. In New York City, and probably elsewhere, teachers of the retarded were taken to be the dumbest teachers; teachers of emotionally disturbed children were often described as having inadequate personalities themselves; teachers in the homebound program were thought to be unequal to the task of managing a group or interacting closely with other professionals. Unfortunately, these associations were probably often not far from wrong. With the shortage of teachers in the 1950s and early 1960s, almost anyone who was willing to work with handicapped children was hired. Given the low status that such positions had in most public school systems, relatively few bright, competent teachers were attracted to teaching disabled children.

The handicapped children in public schools in the 1950s and 1960s were not severely handicapped. Severely handicapped children, when they were educated at all, received their schooling in agency-operated centers. Local branches of the National Association for Retarded Citizens ran some of these centers. Local branches of United Cerebral Palsy operated others. Some centers were affiliated with university medical schools. While a small number of these centers, because of the reputations they established, managed to attract very gifted persons as teachers, most did not. In general, the teachers in these centers were less educated and had poorer records of achievement than most teachers in public school systems.

Perhaps this is as it should be, you might be thinking. Perhaps very bright, innovative individuals would become quickly bored by the limited scope and potential of these children's minds. Perhaps a somewhat duller person who can more readily adjust to the necessary repetition of low-level tasks is more appropriate in the role of teacher of the severely handicapped. Perhaps . . . but I don't really think so.

I started my career as a kindergarten teacher. After one year in this role I was happy to move on to first grade. I had spent about twenty hours a week for nine months "doing homework" for this job and felt that I had mastered the essential elements of teaching kindergarten children. A year later I was getting worried about having to teach first grade again. I knew that I wasn't the best first-grade teacher around, but I had done a pretty good job at it, and the possibility of boredom loomed before me. With great relief, I grabbed at the idea of teaching a class of severely disturbed children the following year. What a challenge! During the next three years in just such a position I was never bored. Exhausted, drained, shook-up, desperate, yes. Bored, never. How can you be bored when you are breaking new ground? How can you be bored when you are dealing with children who can't help you help them? How can you be bored when you have to constantly find or invent new means of reaching them? How can you be bored when you have the most difficult teaching task possible? You can get bored only if you give up on them, only if your own intelligence and ingenuity fail you. Then teaching becomes a monotonous repetition of the obvious. At this point in time, teaching severely disabled children is probably the most challenging teaching assignment there is. The best, the brightest teachers are needed for this task.

P.L. 94-142 calls for the education of all handicapped children from ages 3 to 21. Public education for 3- and 4-year-olds was extremely rare before passage of this law. Many children will be helped by this downward extension of free education, but for some severely handicapped children age 3 is late. Remember Raun (Chapter Three)? If Barry and Susi Kaufman had waited a year and a half or two years for their son's education to begin, they might have lost him to his impenetrable world. At 16 months he was already sliding backwards, just as Josh Greenberg's son Noah did (Chapter Two) between ages 2 and 3. If

Raun had begun a school program at age 3, would the barrier between him and human society have been breached? Perhaps, but surely with much more difficulty. Surely, much more time would have been needed. Possibly, even probably, the fantastic level of development achieved by this little boy, his new potential, could not have been accomplished.

> Raun Kahlil is two-and-a-half years old and continues to soar. He is loving, happy, creative, and communicative. . . . His enjoyment of people remains intense; he can speak in sentences of up to fourteen words. He creates fantasy characters from his imagination. . . . Numbers and counting have worked their way into his world. Favored games include adding and subtracting. Raun Kahlil plays with letters freely and can spell over fifty words.
>
> Raun's energy is matched only by his happiness. (Kaufman, 1976, p. 152)

Barry and Susi Kaufman created their own educational program for their son Raun. It was a beautiful program, infused with love, insight, creativeness, and intensive seven-day-a-week teaching. Few programs can duplicate the richness and intensity of the educational intervention devised by the Kaufmans. Instead of forty-five to seventy-five hours of instruction per week, schools offer twenty-five or less. Instead of three teachers for one child, the ratio may be five children to one teacher. But few children like Raun have parents as gifted and resourceful as the Kaufmans. The alternative for most of these children is still to wait until age 3, even when attentive parents have noted something seriously wrong long before this age. The "Bill of Rights for the Handicapped" is a magnificent document, but for these children it still falls short.

There are of course model programs in which a few infants are lucky enough to find places. Some of these are funded by the U.S. Office of Education, Bureau of Education for the Handicapped. Some are funded by national associations or state agencies. I went to visit one. In a large room stood eight cribs. This was the infant room. A teacher was working on a mat with a child of 5 months, stimulating the baby, attempting to keep its attention, helping it practice simple motor skills. Another child was being held by the director of the center. He was 2, but he was the size of a 9- or 10-month-old. Severly brain-damaged at birth he could not sit, hold his head up, turn over, or swallow solid foods. His 23-year-old mother had been desperate with hopelessness and exhaustion until this program had admitted him. A little girl was holding onto the bars of a crib. As I approached she began to cry loudly. She was afraid of people, I was told. In another crib a baby was asleep on his stomach. He was one of the healthiest looking babies I had ever seen—big and plump, pink-skinned and strong looking. I was delighted and fascinated by this air of health in such a setting. A few minutes later the baby stirred and turned over. His tongue protruded. His nose was broad and flat, his eyes different. This perfect specimen of health had Down's Syndrome! The shock stayed with me all afternoon. Even though I had known that this was a program for retarded infants, I hadn't been prepared. I was still plagued by my stereotypes. I felt somewhat better when I saw a 2-year-old with Down's Syndrome who had learned to feed, toilet, and help dress himself. He had been in the program since he was 6 months old. I felt better when I saw a mother beaming at every small sign of growth in her child, obviously loving her and having hope. I felt better when I noted the playfulness of some of the children, and the affection between adults and children. Good things were happening here and everyone felt it.

MAINSTREAMING

We have a propensity for labels. They are convenient shortcuts, saving us time and energy. But this same convenience creates a problem. A label may arouse different images and associations in different people. Mainstreaming is one such label, and what started out to be a natural implication of current movements and facts is in danger of becoming a disaster.

In a way, Lloyd Dunn started it. He titled a 1968 article "Special Education for the Mildly Retarded—Is Much of It

Justifiable?" It was a rhetorical question. Dunn's answer was "no." His arguments were based on facts as well as theory. Fact: Studies of the educational progress of mildly retarded pupils provide no evidence that special class placement is better than regular class placement. Fact: Studies of the effects of being labeled "mentally retarded" (and then placed in a special class for retarded children) appear to indicate that such labeling is a detriment to the child's self-esteem and social acceptance. Fact: Many of the children placed in special classes for the mildly retarded are children of the poor and children of ethnic minorities. Fact: Many professionals have questioned the validity of the standard diagnostic procedure for labeling a child as mentally retarded if he comes from a racially or economically disadvantaged group. The basic assumption of the standard IQ tests—that all children have had exposure to the general culture from which the test items are drawn—is not true in regard to these children.

> The conscience of special educators needs to rub up against morality. In large measure we have been at the mercy of the general education establishment in that we accept problem pupils who have been referred out of the regular grades. In this way, we contribute to the delinquency of the general educations since we remove the pupils that are problems for them and thus reduce their need to deal with individual differences. The *entente* of mutual delusion between general and special education that special class placement will be advantageous to slow learning children of poor parents can no longer be tolerated. We must face the reality—we are asked to take children others cannot teach, and a large percentage of these are from ethnically and/or economically disadvantaged backgrounds. Thus much of special education will continue to be a sham of dreams unless we immerse ourselves into the total environment of children from inadequate homes and backgrounds and insist on a comprehensive ecological push—with a quality educational program as part of it. (Dunn, 1974, p. 22)

Handicap labels and isolation are not the answer for this problem! Dunn's suggested solution was individualized diagnostic-prescriptive teaching. Special educators, instead of working with self-contained classes of retarded children, would serve as resource teachers for all children with learning problems in regular classes. They would identify each child's special needs and develop individual programs. The programs would be in part implemented by the special educator in a resource room in the school, but would for the most part be implemented by the classroom teacher. Labels and isolation could be reduced drastically. Many children could again become part of the mainstream.

It was an intelligent, humanistic proposal. The time was ripe for it. Other leaders in special education were grappling with this problem. In the same year Evelyn Deno (1968) introduced a model for a cascade system of educational services, a model that was to become a blueprint for planning after it appeared in an article in the journal *Exceptional Children* in 1970. This model highlights the various alternatives for handicapped children as levels along a continuum pointing toward the goal of standard educational programming. Special class placement is only one of several alternatives, Deno reminded us. There are more desirable alternatives (Levels I–III in the figure) for most mildly disabled children.

Inherent in the Deno model was the concept of "least restrictive environment." The concept of least restrictive environment implied that

> to the maximum extent appropriate, handicapped children . . . are educated with children who are not handicapped, and that special classes, separate schooling, or other removal of handicapped children from the regular education environment occurs only when the nature and severity of the handicap is such that education in regular classes with the use of supplementary aids and services cannot be achieved satisfactorily. (Public Law 93-380, Title VIB, Sec. 612[d] [13b])

I went to see some children in a high school program based on the concept of "least restrictive environment." This was a high school which the New York City Board of Education touted as a model of what should be. It was a nice school, two years old, clean and comfortable. The sense of comfort came from more than the physical structure. It was apparent in the lack of bells to signal the change of classes, in the relaxed way in which both students and teachers moved, and in the quiet hum in the hallways.

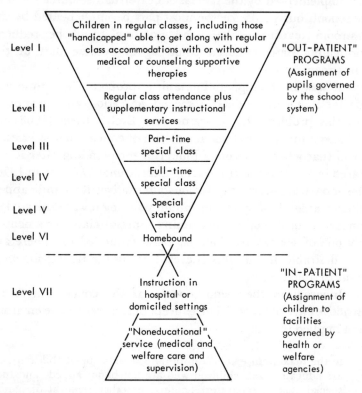

Figure 6-1 The cascade system of special education service. The tapered design indicates the considerable difference in the numbers involved at the different levels and calls attention to the fact that the system serves as a diagnostic filter. The most specialized facilities are likely to be needed by the fewest children on a long-term basis. This organizational model can be applied to development of special education services for all types of disability. SOURCE: From E. Deno, "Special Education as Developmental Capital," in G. J. Warfield, ed., *Mainstream Currents.* Reston, Va.: The Council for Exceptional Children, 1974, p. 66. Reprinted by permission of The Council for Exceptional Children.

The coordinator of the special education program would be back in his office shortly. Would I have a seat, the young woman asked. She was a teacher-aide and physically handicapped. Mr. Z.[1] came in a minute later. He talked about the program's goals, its accomplishments, what he hoped to do the following year. He was obviously dedicated and sensitive. We began a tour. There were 156 young people receiving special education services in this school of 1,300 students, but it was hard to find them. There were no homerooms in which they might be gathered. Each student's program was individualized. Most of the 156 students took five of their seven daily periods in regular classes. We visited some resource rooms where the special education students come for individualized help. A visually impaired boy took a history test as his resource teacher read the questions aloud to him. A boy with cerebral palsy who couldn't control his hand movements well enough to write legibly or type, dictated a paper. Two other boys would arrive shortly for help in deciphering their social studies reading assignments. They had been referred to the school as neurologically impaired. We moved on. Two children out of 156. Where were the rest? The coordinator stopped a boy in the hallway and introduced us. The young man's speech told me immediately that he was number three of the 156. I had to listen carefully to understand what he was saying. He was wearing a leg brace for the first time and now he could walk straight, he 'told us. This was the boy whose mother had called Mr. Z. earlier, I realized. She had been concerned about how her son would react to wearing the brace, and wanted Mr. Z. to be aware of the situation. He was doing fine, mother. I turned and watched the boy walk away. The outline of the brace on his left leg was barely visible through the material of his pants. This multiply handicapped boy hadn't been visible to me as anything but another student in the hall until we had stopped him.

"What about the retarded?" I asked. "Are they too now moving individually from class to class, mingling with the

---

[1]Mr. Z. is Allen H. Zelon, Coordinator of the Special Education Program at Edward R. Murrow High School, New York City.

general student body?" "Probably not," Mr. Z. replied. (The irony of Dunn's contribution is that it may be working better for children with other kinds of disabilities than for the retarded.) We stopped at the door of a classroom where about twelve students were listening to a teacher. This was an academic class for retarded students. A few black faces stared out at us. The retarded students generally take all their academic work with other retarded children, Mr. Z. was saying. They do take some classes in the mainstream—shop, gym and a couple of others—but most of these children spend five out of their seven daily pro-grammed periods in special education classes. "At this level it's hard to do anything else," Mr. Z. mused. "Perhaps with younger children. . . ." Still a problem. Too many black faces, too much isolation. He is trying something, though. Some of the mildly retarded students are in remedial reading and remedial math classes set up for the general student population. At least they are getting contact with some of the general student population this way. We looked in on such a remedial math class. About ten young men were working at their desks while a male teacher put examples on the blackboard. No one "looks retarded." White and black faces look up.

Another resource room. A girl in a wheelchair. No in-visibility here. The girl's arms cut through the air in angular motions. Cerebral palsy with severe motor impairment. I noted that the girl was wearing the school "uniform"—jeans, sneakers, and a picture T-shirt. Just then two other students appeared. It was time to change classes. One girl took charge of the wheelchair while the other one picked up books. But before they moved out of the room one of the girls bent down and greeted her friend with a kiss on the forehead.

"We have not had to assign personnel to transport students from class to class," Mr. Z. said. "Every student who needs help seems to attract his or her own circle of willing helpers. They work out the arrangements themselves. This is the first time Sue's ever been in contact with nondisabled people her own age. She's made real friends here. She's been a weekend visitor at the homes of several of the girls in the school. And it isn't because they pity her. She has a good mind. They enjoy her. If you know the physical arrangements that have to be made to have her as a weekend guest, you can sense the depth of these friendships."

I thanked Mr. Z. and said goodbye. Spectacular? No, I thought to myself. I was not left with the impression of great achievements. I wondered that it had not always been this way. This place was as it should be. This was a normal world. Nothing spectacular. Just somehow quietly right. And when you're there, you forget that this is not the way the rest of the world functions. You forget the pains of the past and present.

"Perhaps with younger children," Mr. Z. had said. I went to see. The first place on my list was a state institution for the severely retarded, the last place one would expect to go to see integration, mainstreaming, or the concept of least restrictive environment in operation. From the outside it didn't look like the stereotype of a state institution. It was a series of low buildings alternating with grassy areas. Inside everything was painted in bright yellows and oranges. The nursery school area surrounded a small outdoor yard. There was lots of open space. Play equipment was sturdy, attractive, and plentiful. I went into the 3-year-old group. The room was tiny. In it were six children at play. As I looked carefully, I noted that one child had microcephaly (underdeveloped skull), another had Down's Syndrome, and another was extremely awkward in his movements. A little girl was sitting next to the child with Down's Syndrome, showing him how to put back the pieces of a puzzle. Another child took the hand of the boy with microcephaly, sat him down in a play area, and began to give him toys. Incredible, I thought, here were 3-year-old children of normal intelligence accepting and serving as teachers of their severely retarded peers. It was different in the kindergarten group. There hadn't been any cleavage at the beginning of the year, but slowly, subtly it had occurred. The nonimpaired children had begun to play with other nonimpaired children. They had begun to sit with each other. It was a natural development, based on common interests and competencies, not a sign of prejudice, the director explained. The children showed no hostility or rejection. Eventually, a separate group was formalized for the children who were not retarded.

It had probably been too much to expect. We were talking about severely retarded children. The amazing thing about this experiment was that it had been implemented in the first place, and that it had worked with children of 3 and 4. Something had been gained. Something had been learned. These children were severely retarded and by age 5½ or 6 co-education wasn't working. But, I wondered, what if the retarded children had been 7- or 8-year-olds, two years older than their nonretarded classmates? Would it have worked then? Or what if they had been mildly retarded?

I was referred to a public school in a large city school system. This system was known as being committed to the promotion of mainstreaming. I asked particularly about retarded children. I had already seen mainstreaming working well for children with a variety of mild to moderate physical disabilities. Visually impaired children had been successfully integrated into many school programs for years. Integration of hearing-impaired children was more problematic but great progress was being made in this direction. It was the retarded of Lloyd Dunn's theory that I wanted to see.

Annie was almost 9 and she was in a first-grade class. She had silky, reddish hair and was attractively dressed, but she had the unmistakable features of Down's Syndrome. I watched her sitting in a cluster of desks, copying arithmetic examples from the board, counting on her fingers to figure out the answers, picking out words on a chart, doing puzzles, reading, writing. I watched her playfully tap a little boy who stopped at her desk, and then turn to her neighbor with a question. She wasn't the most popular child in the class, but neither was she the least popular. She wasn't as good as some of the other children in arithmetic, but neither was she the worst. She was, by the way, the best reader. And she loved school.

What about next year when her classmates would be older, when some of the ideas they dealt with in school would be less concrete? Perhaps there would be difficulties. The teacher anticipated some. She was worried also about the reactions of some of the boys toward Annie. They weren't sure she should be continued in a regular class for the full school day. Our fears and doubts do us injustice. They do children injustice.

There is another girl with Down's Syndrome whose name is Kathryn. Her local school system felt that she belonged in a special class. They believed that she was not ready to deal with symbols even after she was already writing with them. They believed that she needed to be in a very small class, even after she had spent several years in classes of more than twenty children. Kathryn is in an open classroom of eighty-three children, in a nearby town. Her classmates are much younger than she, but she loves school, the school loves her, and she has many friends. She reads the same books the other children do and enjoys the same games. What will happen to her as she gets older, as her classmates get older? Her needs will be met in the most appropriate way, just as they are being met in what is now the most appropriate way (Bennett, 1974).

There appear to be different times for different kinds of learning together. There appear to be wide variations in the courage and willingness of educators to explore the outermost boundaries of this union, to push at the barriers, to probe for the points beyond which it cannot go.

PUSHING AT THE BOUNDARIES

We can push at the boundaries that separate children by integrating the able-bodied and the disabled in body, by integrating children with varying degrees and kinds of abilities in schoolrooms across the nation. This is necessary, but it is not enough. We can push at the boundaries that separate children by reaching their minds as well. We can push at these boundaries by reaching the minds of their teachers and principals and parents.

Teachers are members of society and as such they often reflect the values dominant in that society. For many years society dictated that children with all but the mildest of disabilities did not belong in public schools, certainly not in regular classes, mingling with "normal" children. Teachers shared this value, and such values are slow to change. We cannot afford to wait for this change to occur of itself.

The track record of the schools is not good. Children with disabilities are different and they are the same. In the past, schools did little to encourage perception of similarity in terms of a wide range of characteristics; they did little to stimulate enjoyment of differences. Homogeneous classes, ability groupings within classes, rewards for uniformity—all reinforce tendencies that lead to denigration of those with disabilities. When to be valued means to do better than many of one's peers, we are almost by definition degrading most disabled children.

The track record of the schools is not good. Children receive messages of degradation, denigration, and devaluation of the disabled from the physical organization. Classes for the disabled are often in the basement or in an isolated corner off the ground floor where there is little need to venture.

Without awareness, teachers reinforce vague fears and feelings of discomfort about the disabled by such comments as: "Are you deaf? I just told you that"; or "Why is that so hard for you to grasp? Are you retarded?" There is anger or exasperation in their voices when they say this. The association lingers.

The track record of the schools is not good when one looks at curriculum. The cry of blacks in the 1950s and early 1960s can be borrowed. There are few persons with disabilities pictured in children's readers or other instructional materials. The disabled don't exist in this world. There are no references to the treatment of the disabled in the history books our children read; few or no references to disorders of the senses or skeletal system in the science and health education books. Few teachers attempt to deal with the often incidental but negative stereotypes of the disabled in the literature their high school students read. Occasionally Franklin Delano Roosevelt's paralysis is mentioned, or Helen Keller's great achievement, but these are oddities, isolated examples that have no meaning in terms of the people who might exist in everyday life.

Annie's teacher had said to me: "I never had a child like Annie before. I didn't know what to do with her, how to treat her. I was afraid I couldn't control her." Integration is more than physical cohabitation. We need to reach teachers, to broaden their minds, touch their fears. They are the models in our classrooms, and they control the reinforcements.

It could be an exciting venture, like a curtain being slowly drawn open to expose a world that had only been known through vague and frightening shadows before. It could be an experience in growth, an added dimension, a remedial program to alleviate the cultural deprivation of our "normal" childhoods and adulthoods. It could be a new curriculum for our schools, from kindergarten through college.

A NOTE ON SABOTAGE

I was making some concluding remarks at a conference held in the spring of 1975. "I don't usually make predictions about the future," I began, "but unless mainstreaming is accompanied by efforts to sensitize and train teachers, by efforts to deal with the fears, superstitions, and prejudices of children and teachers alike, it will fail. The pendulum will swing back."

There was another caution I voiced at that conference. It had to do with money and resources. Mainstreaming is a very vulnerable concept. It is too easy to use the label without the guts of this idea; too easy to slip children back into regular classes without any special services and still call it mainstreaming. This is not mainstreaming. Mainstreaming is not a way to save money. Unfortunately, some administrators and some boards of education are using this idea in just this way, for just such a purpose. They have devised the ultimate means of sabotage. The word for this procedure is not mainstreaming. The word for this deprivation of special services to children with special needs is already familiar to us. We have seen it in many forms before. It is called dumping, and no amount of fancy talk will turn it into anything else.

REFERENCES

ABESON, A., and J. BALLARD, "State and federal policy for exceptional children," in *Public Policy and the Education of Exceptional Children*, ed. F. Weintraub, A. Abeson, J. Ballard, and M. L. Lavor, pp. 83–85. Reston, Va.: The Council for Exceptional Children, 1976.

BENNET, J. M. "Proof of the Pudding," *The Exceptional Parent*, 4, no. 3 (1974), 8–12.

Children's Defense Fund, *Children Out of School in America*. Cambridge, Mass.: Children's Defense Fund, 1974.

DENO, E., "Educational Aspects of Minimal Brain Dysfunction in Children," *Proceedings of the Sixth Delaware Conference on the Handicapped Child*, pp. 41–65. Wilmington, Del: A. I. Dupont, 1968.

———, "Special Education as Developmental Capital, in *Mainstream Currents: Reprints from Exceptional Children 1968-74*, ed. G. J. Warfield, pp. 60–68. Reston, Va.: The Council for Exceptional Children, 1974.

DUNN, L. M., "Special Education for the Mildly Retarded—Is Much of It Justifiable?", in *Mainstream Currents: Reprints from Exceptional Children 1968-74*, ed. G. J. Warfield, pp. 7–24. Reston, Va.: The Council for Exceptional Children, 1974.

GILHOOL, T. K., "Education: An Inalienable Right," *Public Policy and the Education of Exceptional Children*, ed. F. J. Weintraub et al., pp. 14–21. Reston, Va.: The Council for Exceptional Children, 1976.

KAUFMAN, B. N., *Son Rise*. New York: Harper & Row, 1976.

Public Law 93-380 (Education Amendments of 1974), 1974.

TIDYMAN, E., *Dummy*. New York: Bantam Books, 1975.

SEVEN

Access

A disabled person was asked what changes took place in his life as a result of becoming physically disabled. He said:

> The main difference is the loss of spontaneity in your life. . . .
> You might be sitting around the house in the evening and you or
> your wife or somebody might say, "Gee, let's go out for a pizza."
> . . . If you're disabled, you really have to have a fully worked out
> battle plan just to go out to get a pizza, drink a little beer. . . .
> You have to know which pizza parlor is accessible, that you can
> get into; which pizza parlor might have parking spaces which if
> you park in them, you can get your wheelchair out of. If you plan
> to have a little beer with your pizza, you want to know which pizza
> parlor has accessible rest rooms. . . . You just don't all-of-a-
> sudden do anything. Everything has to be thought out and planned
> in advance. (Jones and Farr, 1975, 1975, Tape #1)

SLOWLY THE BARRIERS FALL

An organization of disabled students had lobbied for several months to make their college building accessible to those in wheelchairs. The major change to be made was the addition of a ramp to supplement the steps at the main entrance. Finally the ramp was finished. A ribbon-cutting ceremony was scheduled, with the president of the college set to do the honors. Just before the ceremony, a student in a wheelchair who was to demonstrate the function of the ramp made a trial run. He moved slowly to the top of the first part of the narrow ramp and then attempted to make the turn to the second part. He tried over and over again. The space provided was insufficient. The ceremony was canceled. The ramp was quickly redesigned and rebuilt. Several weeks later the ceremony was again scheduled. This time the student did negotiate the ramp in his wheelchair. What most of the spectators applauding this scene did not realize was that when the disabled student finally got to the top of the ramp still another barrier faced him. The doors to the building were too heavy for a person in a wheelchair to manage. When someone in a wheelchair gets to the top of that ramp and moves the few feet to the door of the building, he has to stop and wait. In rain and snow and hot summer days, he waits for someone who can walk to open the door for him. The disabled are making progress, but at almost every step of the way there is another battle, another disappointment, another barrier.

In the United States today it is estimated that one out of ten persons has limited mobility due to a temporary or permanent physical disability. Improved medical techniques and an expanding population of older persons is increasing this number every year. Yet in general, the physical environment of our Nation's communities continues to be designed to accommodate the ablebodied, thereby increasing the isolation and dependence of disabled persons. To break this pattern requires a national commitment. (National Center for a Barrier Free Environment, 1974)

If the handicapped cannot enter and use public buildings, they cannot easily vote, obtain government services, conduct business, or become independent and self-supporting. Efforts to enhance talents and market job skills become meaningless when the job site and usual places of business are inaccessible. (Comptroller General of the United States, 1975, p. 1)

Figure 7-1   International symbol of access for the handicapped. A symbol is a sign by which one infers a thing, an object used to represent something abstract. As recognized around the world, the international symbol of access represents the hope of independence and mobility to handicapped persons. Wherever it is displayed, the handicapped can be assured that they will not be barred by thoughtless obstacles or prohibited from participating in the mainstream of society ("People Are Asking About . . . Displaying the Symbol of Access," p. 11).

In 1961 a major step was taken toward facing the problem of inaccessibility of the man-made environment for physically disabled persons. The President's Committee on the Employment of the Handicapped, together with the National Easter Seal Society for Crippled Children and Adults, and the American Standards Association, had undertaken a project to develop standards for making buildings accessible to the disabled. In 1961 they issued the product of their collaboration — *The American National Standard Specification for Making Buildings and*

Facilities Accessible to and Usable by the Physically Handicapped.

What were these standards? What did they involve? They involved ramps and walks, parking lots and building entrances, doorways and floors. These standards concerned people in wheelchairs being able to get into buildings, and once there, being able to use toilet facilities, or get a drink from a water fountain, or use a public telephone. They concerned people having restricted mobility being able to negotiate stairs. They concerned blind persons who could not read danger signs, and deaf persons who could not hear audible warnings, such as fire bells. The standards involved no drastic departures from good conventional planning. Nor were they terribly expensive. It has been estimated that the additional cost to a builder of meeting the 1961 standards was approximately one-tenth of one percent of the total cost of a new building.

The document embodying these new standards was widely disseminated. It was a time of optimism. Now that standards had been developed for making buildings accessible, now that it could be shown that the cost would not be prohibitive and that no one would be inconvenienced by the changes, surely a new era of accessibility would be ushered in.

Several disappointing years followed. At the local government level, little progress was noted in making new public facilities accessible. While there were some signs of progress at the state level (by 1965 twenty-four states had taken legislative action designed to eliminate architectural barriers from public buildings), state laws were often discretionary or not comprehensive. At the federal level, there was still no directive to insure the elimination of barriers in government-funded building projects, and inaccessible facilities were still being erected. Standards alone were not enough. Another step had to be taken. Congress acted. The Architectural Barriers Act of 1968 was passed.

The purpose of the Architectural Barriers Act was "to insure that certain buildings financed with federal funds are so designed and constructed as to be accessible to the physically handicapped" (First Report of the Architectural and Transportation Barriers Compliance Board, 1974, p. 145). Specifically covered were buildings and facilities owned or leased by the government, or constructed with the assistance of federal funds. The 1961 standards were adopted by federal agencies as mandatory specifications. Accessibility for the physically handicapped was public policy at last.

Minimal standards had been established. Laws had been passed. The time for implementation had arrived. Again the results were disappointing. In the second half of 1974 the United States General Accounting Office inspected 314 buildings constructed, altered, or leased by the federal government after passage of the Architectural Barriers Act of 1968. The conclusion of this evaluation was that "the Architectural Barriers Act had had only a minor effect on making public buildings barrier free." Moreover, "buildings currently being designed and constructed are only slightly more barrier free than buildings designed and constructed within the years immediately after passage of the act" (Comptroller General of The United States, 1975, p. 6). Of the 314 buildings surveyed, there was 98 percent noncompliance in regard to restrooms; 91 percent in regard to parking lots, doors, and doorways; 90 percent in regard to warning signals (Ibid., p. 229). There was a long, hard battle still ahead, and the disabled knew it.

If you have taken any part in seeing legislation that attempts to give citizens with disabilities an even chance to "share in America's bounty" become "the law of the land," DO NOT RELAX! In the name of ignorance or lack of time, money, and personnel, government on all levels is our major law breaker. It is up to us, individually and collectively, to stay alert, point out oversights with tenacity, and generally be a reminder. (Zlotnick, 1975, p. 72)

The battle goes on. It will for years. There are still tens of thousands of buildings which people in wheelchairs cannot enter without being carried like babies. These are buildings they must enter if they are to assume full membership in society. They include schools and banks, museums and law courts, libraries, shopping centers, and office buildings. Nor will the fight end there. With time, the term "accessible" will take on a more stringent meaning. No longer will it include buildings that are accessible by dint of freight elevators and circuitous pathways. "Accessible" will come to mean structures that disabled persons can get into and move around in the way other people do, in the same elevators, down the same halls. A disabled person "shouldn't have to go clear around the building and come back in and go up the freight elevator to the 8th floor if a guy on two legs doesn't have to do that" (*Progress Toward a Barrier-Free Environment*, 1974, p. 39).

GETTING THERE

The problem is not only how to get into buildings, or what one can do inside buildings after entering them. It is also how to get *to* those buildings. Whether one thinks of "walking," taking a bus, using a subway, or getting a plane, there is a barrier in each path.

> If president-elect Franklin D. Roosevelt, traveling in 1933 from Hyde Park, New York, to Washington, D.C. for his inauguration, had been forced to rely solely on ordinary transportation services, he would not have arrived. He could not have walked up the steps of a bus or train. If he had chosen to fly, he probably would have been denied passage unless he had an able-bodied companion with him. Once in Washington, he would have found not only more inaccessible buses, but also a fleet of taxi drivers reluctant to pick up a wheelchair passenger.

> Today a similarly disabled person would encounter the same obstacles on a journey to almost any city in the United States. ("Accessible Transportation: A Critical Issue," 1976, p. 10)

There are over 400,000 persons in this country who live in

wheelchairs. Where can they go? If they try to take a "walk" through their neighborhoods, chances are that it will turn out to be a very short walk. Their walk will probably end at the first intersection. While some disabled veterans have learned to do all kinds of wheelchair acrobatics, including curb jumping, the same curb that we step off without thinking is as effective a barrier to most people in wheelchairs as a brick wall would be to those whose legs are not damaged. With few exceptions, neither public buses nor city subways are accessible to those in wheelchairs. Only infrequently will taxis take wheelchair passengers. The majority of physically disabled persons, many of them aged and unable to work, do not have the resources to purchase and operate their own cars. The prison bars around many of those who live in wheelchairs do not produce images on the retinas of our eyes. These prison bars have to be seen by our minds.

Does it have to be this way? Is there no alternative? What crime did the physically disabled commit that they should be so punished? The "crime" committed by many disabled persons is becoming old.

The life expectancy of our population today is approximately seventy years. That life expectancy will increase even further during the next few years. One out of every two persons over 65 suffers some limitation of mobility. Not all of these elderly persons with mobility limitations live in wheelchairs. Many use walkers or canes. Some attempt to manage as in their former days, with no special aids. What they all have in common is deteriorating agility, speed, and coordination. The poverty of many of our citizens over 65 makes it essential for them to use public transportation if they are to continue to move out into the environment. It is essential if they are to meet even such basic needs as medical care.

What do people over 65 tell us about the appropriateness of public transportation for them? A study of retired persons, many of them still under 65, revealed that 77 percent of the respondents were afraid of falling on public buses. Twenty percent had actually fallen, and a majority of respondents had witnessed someone else fall. They were afraid of the fast-closing doors, of getting on and off those steep steps, of the speed of starts and stops. Older people have poorer balance. They are more likely to fall; and having fallen, they are more likely to be seriously hurt. The 1971 White House Conference on Aging identified transportation as the third major problem of the elderly (*Progress Toward a Barrier-Free Environment*, pp. 12–14).

Physical disability is a minority problem among the young and middle-aged, but among those who reach the life expectancy age of 70 it is a problem of the majority. A very small percentage of us will experience loss of mobility because of diseases like multiple sclerosis or muscular dystrophy; a somewhat larger, but still small percentage, will experience this loss because of accidents; most of us, however, will become old.

The Urban Mass Transportation Act of 1964 makes it national policy that

> Elderly and handicapped persons have the same right as other persons to utilize mass transportation facilities and services; . . . special efforts shall be made in the planning and design of mass transportation facilities and services so that the availability to elderly and handicapped persons of mass transportation which they can effectively utilize will be assured. . . . (First Report of the Architectural and Transportation Barriers Compliance Board, 1974, p. 53)

It is good that a national policy on rights for the physically limited has been established. It is a much more complex problem to fulfill this policy. The technology is there. Models have been developed. Low floors, nonskid surfaces, more grip bars, and wide doors would be helpful to everyone. Ramps and lifts for those in wheelchairs are feasible. What's holding back the forces of change? Money, probably. Attitudes, undoubtedly. The elderly and the disabled want integrated services; they do not want to be isolated into special facilities; but most of us would prefer not to have to see them close up. We are also in a hurry. We become annoyed at a few extra seconds of time spent on a bus ride. The elderly need more time to enter and to leave. A wheelchair lift would mean a few extra seconds on a bus.

The federal government has revved up the engines for change with development and demonstration grants, but somehow it has been afraid to make that final move to set the wheels into motion on a life-size scale. Plans and designs lie somewhere in the offices of the Urban Mass Transportation Administration in Washington, while disabled persons and their friends fight to bring them to life. Organizations of the disabled are crying foul and claiming sabotage ("Accent Update," 1976, p. 23).

A mother of a 12-year-old boy with spina bifida told me about her son's wish to use a subway. The subway seemed to him to be such an integral part of everyone's life. His father took it to get to work. Other boys took it to go to ball games. His mother used it to get to department stores. Yet he didn't really know what it was like. He had seen subways on television but he had never experienced a subway for himself. They wanted to give him this experience, his mother explained, but he was a heavy boy and his father had a bad back. They were really afraid to try to get him and his wheelchair down those steep steps and up again afterwards. How many times I had silently cursed those same New York City subways, sweat boxes in summer, damp and drafty in winter, dirty, crowded, dangerous. But to this 12-year-old boy they were something important, something he was missing out on.

COME FLY WITH ME?

"Fly the friendly skies . . ." began a popular airline commercial of the early 1970s. If the disabled had written their own commercial about the airlines it might have begun: "Try us. You never know. We might be nice today."

Helen Jones (Jones and Farr, 1975, Tape #4) reports a typical example. She, her disabled husband, and their two daughters had flown to Boston on a TWA plane. No difficulties had been encountered. Her husband, a quadriplegic, had returned home alone a week before the rest of the family, again encountering no difficulties. But when Helen Jones attempted to board a TWA plane for the return flight, the picture was different. As she recounts the episode, she was escorted to the entrance of the plane in her wheelchair, and then:

> The attendant stuck out his arm as if to assist me, you know, I should get up and start walking on. And he was astonished when I told him I couldn't walk. You know, I don't know why he thought I was sitting in this wheelchair. And so he called the pilot and all kinds of officials and they refused to let me fly. This is the same airline that had flown my disabled husband home a week earlier, who had flown us all out to the east coast a couple of weeks prior to this. My children were already boarded and seated and they refused to let me go on.

Eventually, after much hassling, Helen Jones was boarded, but this was not the end of it. When the plane arrived in San Francisco she waited and waited to be helped off. Finally, the manager for TWA in San Francisco came aboard and reported that they had no way of getting her off the plane. They didn't have a boarding chair, and the attendants refused to carry her off to her wheelchair. After more puzzlement and pondering the manager, a small man, carried her off on his back because he couldn't think of any other solution. How did Helen Jones, mother and professional "enabler" to other disabled persons, feel about this trip? "It was mortifying. . . ." (Jones and Farr, 1975, Tape #4).

The major problem of air transportation for disabled people is unpredictability. Whether a person who is physically disabled will have a pleasant trip, a painful trip, or no trip at all depends upon factors that are often beyond his control. "Let us know that you are disabled so that we can arrange for your special needs," is the kind of statement made by most major airlines, but the disabled tell it differently.

> Some airlines have not been very friendly to disabled passengers in the past. Many persons have tales of being "bumped" from a flight because a pilot ot ticket agent determined that they were not able to fly because of their physical condition, or because there was no attendant accompanying them, or because they couldn't get to their seats by themselves. . . .
>
> Handicapped persons have sent many complaints to the FAA [Federal Aviation Administration] and the CAB [Civil Aeronautics Board] in recent years about airlines' inconsistent policies and poor treatment of disabled passengers. ("New Rules Coming from FAA for Disabled Passengers," 1974, pp. 26–27)

The inconsistency of treatment of disabled persons by the airlines stems from a lack of definitive regulations coupled with the traditional societal stance of exclusion of the disabled from the mainstream. The Federal Aviation Act of 1958 states that "any air carrier is authorized to refuse transportation to a passenger . . . when, in the opinion of the carrier, such transportation would or might be inimical to safety of flight" (Department of Transportation, 1974). This statement was used by the airlines and their employees to justify the rejection of the disabled as passengers.

In December of 1962 the Air Traffic Conference of America approved a resolution on "Carriage of the Physically Handicapped." This resolution, as written in the Trade Practice Manual of this association of airlines, contained a troublesome provision.

> Persons who cannot take care of their physical needs should not be transported unless, by previous arrangement, a suitable attendant accompanies them. (Schleichkorn, 1972, p. 35)

In addition, this resolution claimed the right of each airline to reject disabled passengers on any particular flight if it was the judgment of airline personnel that the number of disabled persons applying for a particular flight would constitute a safety hazard.

The uncertainty of service and the burdens on the disabled passenger were maintained and formalized. How was one to know when a ticket agent or pilot might decide that there were too many disabled persons for a particular flight? Where were these attendants to come from? Who was to pay for their airline seats?

> When Ralph Markward booked passage on a Texas International Airlines flight from here to Albuquerque, New Mexico, recently, the airline told him he had to buy two seats — one for himself and one for an "attendant."[1]

Even more importantly, did Ralph Markward or many of the other physically disabled persons refused passage without "a suitable attendant" really need one? "No," is the answer that many of the disabled are giving.

In 1973 the Federal Aviation Administration, recognizing the need for new procedures, gave "Advance Notice of Proposed Rule Making" on air transportation of handicapped persons. Questions about attendants were asked. Questions about limiting the numbers of disabled persons on individual flights were asked. Questions about evacuation in emergencies were asked. Hearings were held in six cities. Many persons with disabilities testified. So did representatives of the Airline Pilots Association, which was supporting the continuation of the practice of requiring attendants and limiting the numbers of nonambulatory persons on any one flight. A proposal for new rules was formulated. There was widespread dissatisfaction with it. It was rewritten and then rewritten again. In July of 1976, two years after the proposed new rules were first published in the *Federal Register,* they were still being written. It isn't an easy task. Maybe time is part of the answer, but not much more time, I hope.

---

[1]R. Lindsey, "Travel Woes of Crippled Stirring National Concern," *New York Times,* November 28, 1971, p. V 17. © 1971 by The New York Times Company. Reprinted by permission.

In the meantime planes are flying and disabled persons are using them with varying results. A physician and a lawyer, both physically disabled, were talking about their hassles with the airlines. The lawyer said:

> I can intellectually browbeat these people to get me on an airline. But what about the people who don't have the knowledge and the orientation that I have, and are afraid to call the press and to argue with the managers and to get out in front of the aircraft itself and stop it from taking off if necessary? *Progress Toward a Barrier-Free Environment*, 1974, p. 30)

What about them?

REFERENCES

"Accent Update," *Accent On Living*, 20, no. 4 (1976), 23-26.

"Accessible Transportation," *Amicus*, 1, no. 2 (1976), 8-11.

American National Standard Specifications for Making Buildings and Facilities Accessible To, and Usable By, the Physically Handicapped. New York: American National Standards Institute, 1961.

Comptroller General of the United States, *Report to the Congress: Further Action Needed to Make All Public Buildings Accessible to the Physically Handicapped.* Washington, D.C.: United States General Accounting Office, 1975.

Department of Transportation, "Air Transportation of Handicapped Persons," *Federal Register,* July 5, 1974 (39 F.R. 24667).

First Report of the Architectural and Transportation Barriers Compliance Board. Washington, D.C.: U.S. Department of Health, Education and Welfare, 1974.

JONES, H., and D. FARR, *Realities of the Physically Handicapped.* Tulsa, Okla.: Instructional Media Incorporated, 1975. (audio cassette)

LINDSEY, R., "Travel Woes of Crippled Stirring National Concern," *New York Times,* November 28, 1971, V 17.

National Center for a Barrier-Free Environment (brochure). Washington, D.C.: National Center for a Barrier Free Environment, 1974.

"New Rules Coming from FFA for Disabled Passengers," *Accent On Living*, 18, no. 4 (1974), 26–30.

People Are Asking About . . . Displaying the Symbol of Access (brochure). Washington, D.C.: The President's Committee on Employment of the Handicapped, undated.

Progress Toward a Barrier-Free Environment. Walnut Creek, Cal.: Easter Seal Society for Crippled Children and Adults of Contra Costa County, 1974.

SCHLEICHKORN, J. S., *Carriage of the Physically Handicapped on Domestic and International Airlines.* New York: United Cerebral Palsy Associations of New York State, Inc., 1972.

ZLOTNICK, P. D., "Eye on Congress," *Accent On Living*, 20, no. 3 (1975), 72–73.

EIGHT

The Disabled and the Media

The problem is not that in its 25-year history television has portrayed the disabled child or adult cruelly, mockingly or insensitively. The problem is that it has not portrayed them.*

Fortunately, this statement, which was true in 1973, is becoming much less true today. Fortunately, because television is a powerful tool which the disabled need on their side.

Television probably has the strongest effect upon children. The average child spends twenty to twenty-six hours a week watching it. Numerous research studies have shown that the social attitudes and behavior of young children can be influenced by television viewing (Gorn, Goldberg, and Kanungo, 1976; Liebert, Neale, and Davidson, 1973). "Sesame Street" was probably the most ballyhooed children's television program of the 1960s and 1970s, and it was the program on which much of this research focused. Perhaps this is why the exclusion of children with disabilities from this program was so disturbing.

*From "Television and the Disabled: Mr. Rogers Shows How," *The Exceptional Parent*, 3, no. 1 (1973), 39–41.

In November 1971, a letter¹ (see below) was sent from the editors of *The Exceptional Parent,* a magazine devoted to help-

The
Exceptional
Parent

P.O. Box 101
Back Bay Annex
Boston, Mass. 02117

PUBLISHED BY THE PSY-ED CORPORATION

EDITORS
Lewis B. Klebanoff, Ph.D., S.M.Hyg.
Stanley D. Klein, Ph.D.
Maxwell J. Schleifer, Ph.D.

EDITORIAL ADVISORY BOARD
Burton Blatt, Ed.D.
T. Berry Brazelton, M.D.
Michael S. Dukakis, LL.B.
Gunnar Dybwad, J.D.
Herbert J. Grossman, M.D.
Goodwin D. Katzen
Albert T. Murphy, Ph.D.
Barbara-Jeanne Seabury, M.A.
Harold Turner, D.D.S.

November 1, 1971

Mr. David Connell, Executive Producer
Children's Television Workshop
1865 Broadway
New York, New York 10023

Dear Mr. Connell:

The contemporary phenomenon which is "Sesame Street" has been an exciting stimulus to us all. The immediacy of its impact and the extensive commentary and written reaction it has elicited have had ramifications far beyond the series itself. Your rapid success, extensive exposure and considerable public financial support place upon you signal community responsibilities.

We have special concern for the six million school age children and one million pre-schoolers with disabilities and for the struggle faced by these youngsters and their families not only in finding adequate services for their special needs, but in finding daily acceptance of them as people. Disabled people are also able people and they are defined by their disabilities only in a society which prevents their "normality" from being perceived because of stereotyping and exclusion from the mainstream. This exclusion is harmful and painful to the child with a disability who, for example, if he cannot relate to "Sesame Street," may fall further behind his non-impaired peers. It also segregates the non-disabled child and denies him an important learning experience—the understanding that the variability of people includes not only race but physical, emotional and intellectual characteristics as well.

We feel that exposure to disability will help to make it less mysterious and frightening to non-disabled children. To see other children endure discomfort and/or limitation on a daily basis can be enlightening. To see and help other children persevere and transcend disability can be inspiring. You have the opportunity to make this additional contribution to the social attitudinal education of your viewers.

Obviously, we do not hold you accountable for society's prejudices but we do recognize "Sesame Street's" unique power to effect positive change in them by reaching our youngest, most impressionable citizens. We would, therefore, urge upon you and your colleagues the inclusion of a child with a noticeable disability as a resident of "Sesame Street." We know that, should you accept this recommendation, you will treat him with dignity. We do wish to underline the importance of a direct, non-patronizing depiction of his struggle for recognition, acceptance and competence. It may well be that your contributions to the attitude formation of young children will ultimately outweigh your impact upon cognitive development.

Sincerely yours,

cc: Elliot L. Richardson, Secretary
Department of Health, Education & Welfare
Senator Harrison Williams, Jr., Chairman
Labor and Welfare Committee
Representative Carl D. Perkins, Chairman
Committee on Education and Labor
Sidney P. Marland, Commissioner
U.S. Office of Education
Betram S. Brown, M.D., Director
National Institute of Mental Health
Edward F. Zigler, Ph.D., Director
Office of Child Development
Edwin Martin, Associate Commissioner
Bureau of Education for the Handicapped

Lewis B. Klebanoff, Ph.D., S.M. Hyg.

Stanley D. Klein, Ph.D.

Maxwell J. Schleifer, Ph.D.

¹"A Letter to Children's Television Workshop," *The Exceptional Parent,* 1, no. 3 (1971), 9.

ing parents of the disabled, to the producers of "Sesame Street."
The producers of "Sesame Street" responded.[2]

Dear Editors:

Your letter in the October/November issue of *The Exceptional Parent* arrived at a propitious time. In the new season of "Sesame Street," we have expanded the cast of the show, both adults and children, to expose our audience to a broader spectrum of human interaction. As a part of this expansion, Children's Television Workshop is already investigating how children with noticeable disabilities might become a part of "Sesame Street." As you may know, we have done some work with handicapped children in the past. Last season, we did a program featuring children from The Little Theater of the Deaf and plan a return visit this year.

It's important to remember that "Sesame Street" continues to be an experiment in the use of television for the entertainment and education of preschool children. As such, we are constantly seeking to more effectively achieve our goals. We must move with caution in expanding our goals, however, so the effort is not diluted to the point of losing impact. There is much to be done in preschool education; clearly, we cannot do it all.

With our advisors, we have concluded that trying to teach a tolerance of disabilities on "Sesame Street" is something we should try. I'm not certain that we will go as far with our effort as you would like, nor am I confident that we will be able to measure attitudinal changes as a result of what we do. But we will make a sincere effort.

If you could recommend individuals to us to consult with as we move ahead, we would be anxious to think through the problem with them. We would also welcome your comments about the shows that include disabled children.

Thank you for your kind words about "Sesame Street." Rest assured that all of us at Children's Television Workshop share your concern for the development in our young children of an attitude of total human tolerance.

Sincerely,

David D. Connell

Vice President and Executive Producer

[2]"A Letter to *The Exceptional Parent* from David Connell," *The Exceptional Parent*, 1, no. 4 (1972), 2.

Meetings were held and changes were introduced. Children with cerebral palsy were occasionally included on the program. In the 1975–76 season a special segment designed for mentally retarded children was shown during the first part of each Wednesday's show. Mentally retarded children were featured in these shows, along with the Muppets and other Sesame Street characters. More experiences with the disabled were planned.

Sesame Street had a competitor to catch up to. Fred Rogers, of Mister Rogers' Neighborhood, had long been a friend of disabled children. A mother wrote:

Dear Mr. Rogers:

Thank you for your splendid show, especially for the series you did with Chrissy. Our three-year-old daughter was also born with spina bifida as well as other congenital defects. After her fifth operation last spring and some subsequent complications, she developed some very large fears about walking with her braces and crutches, though she had been able to walk prior to the surgery. Several weeks after watching your "Chrissy shows" and reruns, she asked for her crutches and said "Anne walk for Mr. Rogers." And she did just that. You were the catalyst we needed. (Townley, 1974)

And another, whose 3-year-old adopted son had muscular dystrophy and could not walk, wrote:

When you said you like him, he smiled first and crossed his arms to hug his shoulders. When you said he was "special" he touched his glasses, and looked up at me and nodded he was happy. But then he crossed his arms with a troubled expression on his face and touched his legs. "Legs, Mommy?" he asked. And you answered, you like him just the way he was—he was a special person. Then Jonathan rubbed his knees with his hands and sighed up at me—"Likes me!" "Yes," I answered, "Mister Rogers likes you just the way you are, Jonathan. We all do." ("Television and the Disabled," 1973, p. 40)

"Mister Rogers' Neighborhood" was popular with disabled children and their parents because of the kind of person Fred

Rogers is, long before he began to show special interest in the handicapped. But he did become particularly interested in the handicapped, and in 1972 he embarked on a series of projects with disabled children in mind. First there was the Purple Planet sequence. In a series of five programs, the characters in Mister Rogers' Neighborhood gradually learned to appreciate individual differences. The Purple Planet, a place where everyone was the same, was a very restrictive and boring place, children learned. Differences are to be valued. This opening was followed by programs on which persons with disabilities played major roles. Tim Scanlon, an actor from the National Theatre of the Deaf, was featured as a teacher of mime. Fred Rogers did not, however, shy away from the difficult subject of the speech of deaf people. He told us about it and then asked Tim to talk to us. We heard the stilted rhythm of his speech and its odd inflection, but it was not frightening. Wasn't that Mister Rogers sitting next to Tim, talking to him, enjoying him, and telling us about it?

Chrissy Thompson, mentioned earlier, was a series visitor too. Chrissy has spina bifida. She wears braces and uses crutches. She was introduced to the program as the grandchild of two of the regular characters. She was shown doing things, shown as able. Mister Rogers talked to her television grandparents about her physical impairment. He talked to Chrissy about it too. Even for Fred Rogers this was difficult. As he sat with Chrissy on the steps of a house and talked to her about her braces and special shoes, Fred Rogers, known for his relaxed manner and easy expression, had to struggle to overcome his discomfort and find the right words. The important thing is, of course, that he did.

That's not all. Mister Rogers has embarked upon a new project—development of a series of multi-media packages designed specifically to bolster the self-images, motivation, and skills of young children with disabilities. Mister Rogers has paved the way for the disabled in children's television programming, and in the process he has added a new dimension to his own beauty of person.

Elsewhere on public broadcasting progress was being made

too. "Zoom," an educational television program addressing the 7- to 11-year-old age group, adopted a conscious policy of including disabled children in its guest segments. In a fascinating segment, a deaf boy and his deaf friends talked about what it's like to live in a hearing world. In another segment we watched Timmy, a bright boy who is blind, enjoying his childhood. A third segment helped us understand how a pacemaker can change the life of a child with heart damage.

Action for Children's Television (ACT) became involved too. Americans under 16 spend more time watching television than they do in any activity except sleep (Charren, 1974). ACT was determined that more of this television viewing time would be spent watching something worthwhile, something that developed values beneficial to society. Television violence and advertising abuses were early targets of ACT. Fair representation of the disabled became a target in 1974. ACT's Annual Symposium in 1974 had as one of its four themes "Programming for the Handicapped." Examples of good television programming about the disabled were shown. Unmet needs were identified. One of these unmet needs ACT decided to fill itself — a resource handbook on programming and handicapped children. The handbook was designed as a tool for broadcasters, a guide on enhancing the mutual understanding of handicapped and nonhandicapped children ("ACT Enlists Advisors for its Resource Guide on TV and Handicapped," 1976, p. 3).

There has been lots of action on the public television. The record of commercial television for children, however, has not been as promising. With only a few exceptions, disabled children are still missing from this world. Perhaps that is why a handbook was needed.

Adult programming in which disability is included in either a central or peripheral manner is increasing. Much of it is good. Some of it is bad, strengthening negative stereotypes, reinforcing myths and fears. In the 1970s, favorable but realistic portraits of mildly retarded young adults were presented on "All in the Family" and "Medical Center." A "Marcus Welby" episode dealt sensitively with the prejudice against people with epilepsy. On "Lucas Tanner" the teacher explored reactions to persons who stutter, with his pupils. Blind musicians sang and played, but also talked about their disabilities. We watched the National Theatre of the Deaf perform on public broadcast channels.

Excellent documentaries were presented with increasing frequency. The horrors of Willowbrook, a large state institution for the retarded in Staten Island, New York, were exposed by Geraldo Rivera and a camera. A series of programs examined mental illness. Captions and signing for the deaf became more common. "A Boy Named Timmy Egan" examined the behavior of an autistic child, and his family's reaction to him. "Joey" told the fantastic story of a man so severely impaired by cerebral palsy that he was almost totally helpless; helpless, but not without intelligence. "Joey" was the story of Joseph Deacon as written by him with the help of three of his disabled friends, in the institution where he had spent most of his life, and where someone had finally understood his tortured attempts at speech. So realistic were the portrayals in this story that it was not until almost the end, when the real "Joey" and his actual disabled friends were shown, that I knew for sure that I had been watching actors.

A fresh wind is blowing. Would that it could blow away the frightening stereotypes, both old and new! I remember, still with a chill, the evil mastermind of a series of "Wild, Wild West" episodes around the end of the 1960s. He was a dwarf, and this was no coincidence. Everyone understood that his stature, his punishment from nature, was at the root of his evil nature. This theme, of the disabled turning evil out of bitterness over their misfortune, continues to haunt us. In 1976 on a popular show— Donny and Marie Osmond—during prime family viewing time, Paul Lynde invoked another spectre of destructiveness. With millions of persons watching, many of them children, he mocked the world of a female dwarf. In what was supposed to be a comedy sketch, Paul Lynde, as a real estate salesman, enters the miniaturized home of this tiny lady. The actress in the sketch continued to smile as Mr. Lynde spewed "jokes" at her expense. She must have been a good actress! But much of humor pokes fun at people, you might be thinking. We need to be able to laugh at ourselves. Perhaps we do, but this comedy sketch didn't poke fun at *our* foibles; it poked fun at *them* — people different from us. It accentuated this differentness and then mocked it. We need humor about the disabled. It could help dispel our discomfort and uneasiness about handicaps. But we need humor that exposes the humanness of people with disabilities; not humor that treats them as freaks.

Are you a night owl? If you are, you probably saw plenty of public service announcements about the disabled in the early 1970s. Each time I turned on the television in the early morning hours of a sleepless night I would see one. At 2 A.M., 3 A.M., they were on; at 7 P.M. and 9 P.M., they were not to be seen. If these spot plugs had any effect, we night owls must have been the best informed, most accepting part of the public around in relation to persons with disabilities.

In 1976 a spot announcement appeared on prime television time. It showed a young man talking to his girlfriend, driving a car, holding his books. He was a handsome young man, groomed a la clean-cut American college student. Something was, however, different from the usual TV portrait. This young man had cerebral palsy.

The message was clear. This young man's state government had found him to be a capable driver. An attractive young lady had accepted him as a boyfriend. A college was attesting to his competence as a student. Now it's up to you. He needs your acceptance too.

LITERATURE

Television didn't initiate either the negative portrayals or the exclusion of the disabled in the media. This treatment of the disabled was built into both child and adult literature before television was even invented.

An association between beauty and value is reflected in much of the literature of the past. Children's tales are particularly clear about this. Cinderella was fair of body and spirit, while her mean step-sisters were physically ugly. The creature who threatened the Three Billy Goats Gruff on their way to pasture was "a great ugly Troll, with eyes as big as saucers and a nose as long as a poker" (Hollowell, 1955, p. 68). While Beauty learned to conquer her horror at the sight of the Beast, and eventually learned to love him in spite of his frightening exterior, no sooner did this happen than the Beast was transformed into a handsome Prince. The good Prince was not really ugly! As adults, we can respond to the story of Beauty and the Beast as an allegory, understanding that it was Beauty's perception of the Beast, molded by love, that had changed. We can understand also the repeated message that external appearances are not all that important. But children are literal creatures. While Beauty was a model of humane response to the physically unattractive Beast, the final message of this story to children is a reinforcement of the idea that there is normally a one-to-one correspondence between goodness of soul and perfection of physical form.

When we examine contemporary children's fiction in which disabled characters are included, we find that a majority of these examples are bad—i.e., the conceptual presentation of the disabled character is one that would foster negative beliefs, feelings, and/or behavioral tendencies toward the disabled. Beauty at least controlled her horror at the Beast's appearance and reacted pleasantly to him. In contemporary children's fiction both social rejection and physical violence against the disabled are common (Baskin, 1974).

Why does this kind of thing matter?

> The importance of good books about the handicapped is dual; it is of course desirable for handicapped youngsters to find within books that with which they can identify, but it is equally important for physically normal children to learn intelligent understanding for the handicapped. (Oakley, 1973, p. 58)

> The representation of the handicapped child in literature . . . distorts the capabilities of the disabled . . . frequently dwells on

> cruelties and is excessively melancholy and punitive in tone. . . .
> It seems reasonable to assume that this cumulative effect must con-
> tribute to the exclusionary attitudes so endemic to society.
> (Baskin, 1974, p. 94)

Fortunately, there is a bright side to this story too—there are books for young children, some of them old (for example, *The Little Lame Prince* by Mulock), most of them new, which present a realistic and positive picture of the disabled. (At the end of this chapter there is a selected list of such books.) An increasing number of books for older children and teenagers do the same.

What do most adults read about the disabled? If you're a college graduate, you probably read Greek mythology. Remember Oedipus? His incest was punished by blindness. Message—blindness is a punishment we bring upon ourselves by our sinful behavior. Remember the blind seers? Blind persons were supposed to have super powers. Again, they were presented as being different and apart, although this time better than others. Think of the depiction of physically disabled persons in the literature—the demented Captain Ahab stalking about on his peg leg; Captain Hook, whose prosthetic arm was a menacing weapon; Quasimodo, who was not allowed to live in the company of other people.

In modern adult fiction the disabled hardly exist, unless you want to think of common emotional hang-ups as disabilities. There are, of course, some exceptions. In *To Kill a Mockingbird* (Lee) Bo Radley, a mentally handicapped person, is eventually shown as a hero, but up to this point he is feared and tormented by the neighborhood children, locked in by his parents, accepted by none (Pieper, 1975, p. 116). *Joe Egg* (Nichols) is a play about the desperation of parents of a severely impaired child. *Flowers for Algernon* (Keyes) is the sensitive story of a retarded man who is transformed into a genius for a short time. This trick transfor-mation provides the mechanism for examining reactions to the retarded. The picture is not a happy one. *Light in the Piazza* (Spencer) is a beautiful story of a young girl whose mental development was arrested by a childhood accident. She is eventually accepted in the mainstream of life but only in another social milieu, in a country far from home, with the help of considerable financial resources. *Butterflies Are Free* (Gershe), whose hero is blind, is more joyous. *In This Sign* (Greenberg), about a deaf couple and their daughter, shows the difficult and the possible. But these are specks in an ocean. For the most part there is nothing; probably because we are still afraid or ashamed; perhaps also because we lack imagination.

On the other hand, biographies and autobiographies of the disabled are proliferating. No longer are our choices limited to Helen Keller or Franklin Delano Roosevelt. The National Easter Seal Society for Crippled Children and Adults publishes a list of "Recent Books about Handicapped Persons" (1973). This list includes over 200 biographies. Dozens of blind and orthopedically disabled adults are writing their stories now, sometimes alone, sometimes with help. Magazines are picking up these stories. Newspapers are running others. There is a new receptiveness, and the disabled have discovered words.

Christy Brown can control only the movement of his left foot, but he has senses and a mind. He shared in the life of a Dublin slum with twenty-one brothers and sisters, experiencing its poverty, cruelty, sensuousness, and spirit of adventure. He was carried on his brothers' shoulders, pulled in his home-made cart, used as a rallying point in street fights. Christy Brown never went to school but he absorbed like a hungry sponge, and then, in the ageless tradition of literature, he showed us the meaning of his world.

> He felt the sweat on his forehead trickling down, stinging his eyes; he ached all over with the effort to stand straight and look boldly, stonily ahead. . . . he grunted and shook his head doggedly as his brother tried to wipe some of the sweat from his face. He drew his sagging knees up, lifted his head higher . . . he had refused to remain in the warm-cushioned comfort of the funeral car or even to be driven nearer to where the new grave lay. He had walked with

the others along the endless paths and avenues of the cemetery, supported by two elder brothers, feeling from time to time chill drops of overnight rain drip down onto his bare head and nape from branches drooping along the way.

He had felt good at the start, walking it out with the rest, peacock-proud, even lengthening his jerking stride when his brothers slowed their paces to suit him. As the cortege wound slowly and moved deeper into the desolate acres of Glasnevin his brief triumph ebbed and with each step his muscles and nerves throbbed painfully. A haze swam before his eyes, obscuring the shapes around him. The sweat seeped into his mouth tart and salty. He thrust his head and shoulders forward, a slightly mad dog straining on a fight leash, propelling himself through the cutting wind, shutting his mind to everything save the task of going forward, driving himself on almost past the pitch of feeling pain. He felt every eye focused on him, watching his laboured progress, waiting for him to sink to his knees in the mud. . . .

"We'd better lift him," said one brother to the other. "You take one arm, and I ____"

"You better not, damn you!" he hissed between ragged raging breaths, twisting his face around ferociously.[3]

Christy Brown is alive and he has brought new hope and life to many.

BOOKS ABOUT THE DISABLED FOR CHILDREN

FASSLER, J., *Howie Helps Himself.* Chicago: Albert Whitman & Co., 1975. A picture book about a physically handicapped boy who, like all children, is very proud when he learns to help himself. (Ages 5-7)

HEIDE, F. P., *Sound of Sunshine, Sound of Rain.* New York: Parents Magazine Press, 1970. A poetic picture book told through the thoughts and feelings of a blind child. (Ages 7-9)

HUNTER, E. F., *Child of the Silent Night*. New York: Dell Publishing Co., 1963. The story of Laura Bridgman, a deaf-blind child who was taught to communicate. (Ages 8-10)

KEATS, E. J., *Apt. 3*. New York: Macmillan, 1971. A beautifully illustrated book about two young inner-city boys getting to know a blind man through music. (Ages 6-8)

LASKER, J., *He's My Brother*. Chicago: Albert Whitman & Co., 1974. An attractive picture book about a young learning-disabled child and his problems with friends and school. (Ages 5-7)

LITTLE, J., *Mine for Keeps*. New York: Little, Brown, 1962. A story about a young girl with cerebral palsy, and her adjustment to life in the mainstream. (Ages 8-11)

STEIN, S. B., *About Handicaps: An Open Family Book for Parents and Children Together*. New York: Walker Publishing, 1974. This story of two young friends deals with children's fears about physical handicaps. Accompanying text for adults provides additional ideas for discussion with children. (Ages 5-7)

WOLF, B., *Don't Feel Sorry for Paul*. Philadelphia: J. B. Lippincott, 1974. Photographs and story of a young boy who wears prostheses which enable him to live fully. (Ages 7-10)

REFERENCES

"ACT Enlists Advisors for Its Resource Guide on TV and Handicapped," *Action for Children's Television News* (1976), 3.

BASKIN, B., "The Handicapped in Children's Literature Themes, Patterns and Stereotypes," *The English Record*, 26 (1974), 91-99.

——, "The Handicapped in Children's Literature," in *Fostering Positive Attitudes toward the Handicapped in School Settings*, ed. S. Cohen, pp. 143-64. New York: City University of New York, Special Education Development Center, 1975. (ERIC # ED 115068)

BROWN, C., *Down All the Days*. New York: Stein & Day, 1970.

CHARREN, P. (Sign in), "Children's Television: Some Improvement — Much More Needed," *Signature*, December 1974.

GORN, G. J., M. E. GOLDBERG, and R. N. KANUNGO, "The Role of Educational Television in Changing the Intergroup Attitudes of Children," *Child Development*, 47 (1976), 277-80.

HOLLOWELL, L., *A Book of Children's Literature.* New York: Rinehart, 1955.

"A Letter to Children's Television Workshop," *The Exceptional Parent,* 1, no. 3 (1971), 9.

"A Letter to The Exceptional Parent from David Connell," *The Exceptional Parent,* 1, no. 4 (1972), 2.

LIEBERT, R. M., J. M. NEALE, and E. S. DAVIDSON, *The Early Window: Effects of Television on Children and Youth.* New York: Pergamon, 1973.

National Easter Seal Society for Crippled Children and Adults, selection of recent books about handicapped persons. Chicago: 1973.

OAKLEY, M. C., "Juvenile Fiction about the Orthopedically Handicapped," *Top of the News,* 920 (1973), 57-68.

PIEPER, B., "Some Curricular Experiences for Children," in *Fostering Positive Attitudes toward the Handicapped in School Settings,* ed. S. Cohen, pp. 111-26. New York: City University of New York, Special Education Development Center, 1975. (ERIC#ED 115068)

"Television and the Disabled: Mr. Rogers Shows How," *The Exceptional Parent,* 3, no. 1 (1973), 39-41.

TOWNLEY, R., "Mister Rogers Warm and Wonderful—or Just Plain Dippy?" *The Philadelphia Inquirer,* May 19, 1974.

NINE

Medicine and Technology

The book *Stigma* (Goffman, 1963) began with a letter from Nathanael West's *Miss Lonelyhearts* that is unforgettable.

Dear Miss Lonelyhearts—

I am sixteen years old now and I don't know what to do and would appreciate it if you could tell me what to do. When I was a little girl it was not so bad because I got used to the kids on the block makeing fun of me, but now I would like to have boy friends like the other girls and go out on Saturday nites, but no boy will take me because I was born without a nose—although I am a good dancer and have a nice shape and my father buys me pretty clothes.

I sit and look at myself all day and cry. I have a big hole in the middle of my face that scares people even myself so I can't blame the boys for not wanting to take me out. My mother loves me, but she crys terrible when she looks at me.

What did I do to deserve such a terrible bad fate? Even if I did do some bad things I didn't do any before I was a year old and I was born this way. I asked Papa and he says he doesn't know, but that maybe I did something in the other world before I was born or that maybe I was being punished for his sins. I don't believe that because he is a very nice man. Ought I commit suicide?

Sincerely yours,

Desperate[1]

The questions raised by the 16-year-old girl who signed herself "Desperate" are the kind that every person with a physical deformity asks. "Why me?" questions will continue to be asked and to go unanswered; but for the girl who wrote that letter there is an answer. What medical science has done in recent years for children whose faces were deformed is hardly short of "the work of Gods." Facial features have been constructed, reconstructed, and rearranged. The cruel results of fires and car crashes as well as congenital anomalies have been undone. Doctors have literally broken almost all of the bones of the face and then put them together again in arrangements that can be recognized as human.

Can you imagine what it is like to watch every new person react to you with involuntary shudders, to know that he or she is perceiving you as a monster? Can you imagine what it means to such a child to look "normal," to glance at people and have their eyes return the look without shock and revulsion? Medical science can make this difference; it is doing marvelous things for persons with disfigurements. Plastic surgery is not just a divertissement of medicine that serves our vanities.

[1]Nathanael West, *Miss Lonelyhearts*. Copyright 1933 by Nathanael West; © 1960 by Laura Perelman. Reprinted by permission of New Directions Publishing Corporation.

MODERN MAGIC AND
THE PHYSICALLY DISABLED

Can a quadriplegic move about independently? Can he feed himself, turn the pages of a book, switch on a light? A few years ago the answer to these questions would have been "No, of course not. A quadriplegic is completely dependent upon others." Today, this isn't the answer any more. While most quadriplegics do remain completely dependent upon others, some are now, for the first time in their lives, doing for themselves. One of the finest examples of the use of science and engineering to better the quality of life is the mouth-operated electric wheelchair now being perfected. Such chairs will take adults out of the hospital or institution beds in which they have been largely confined for years and allow them to move into the outside environment. These chairs will mean that the hundreds of young people who will become quadriplegics because of automobile or driving accidents in the next few years will not need to wait for someone to push them, but will be able to choose the direction in which they will move. And sophisticated, mouth-operated electronic devices are being designed to allow the quadriplegic to perform multiple functions from his bed by varying his breathing patterns. By puffing or sipping into a tube, a person who cannot use his hands will be able to answer a telephone and dial a call; turn his radio, TV, lamp on or off; operate a typewriter; open a door. One such device allows a person to perform forty-four separate functions (Rusk, 1975, p. 246). By a combination of puffs and sips a quadriplegic who has no use of his arms or hands may be able to drive a van. This is modern magic, the magic of technology at its best!

Some of the best minds in our country are working on the problem of enlarging functioning in the physically disabled.

Space engineers have developed a wheelchair that can literally be told what to do. . . . The patient wears a microphone to tell the chair what to do. The chair uses a miniature computer that will accept one-word commands such as ready, go, stop, left, right, forward and backward. It has a 32-word memory. ("Wheelchair Follows Orders," 1975, p. 31)

Wheelchairs with arms! Voice-operated, head-operated, chin-operated manipulator arms fitted to wheelchairs; not yet ready for commercial production, but demonstrated as feasible. Space engineers are working together with Veterans Administration prosthetics specialists in one of the valuable fallouts of the space program. This is American technological genius showing itself at its best.

Celeste Thomspon sits in an electric wheelchair. She slightly turns her head, and with her tongue, begins tripping toggle switches held in a bracket near her mouth. In response, an elaborate mechanical brace begins to carry her arm in a sequence of deliberate motions that copy the actions of a normally functioning arm. Celeste Thompson is paralyzed from the neck down. "Rancho Arm Operated by Tongue," 1974, p. 44)

Celeste Thompson contracted polio when she was 19 years old. She spent two years on her back and nine years in a standard wheelchair. She couldn't move herself. Now, with the help of her mechanical arm brace, she picks up cups of coffee, writes letters to friends, types, applies lipstick and mascara.

Mouth-operated electronic devices can provide the severely physically disabled individual with greater control over his life, but bio-engineering may improve the person's ability to control his limbs. Electronic nerve stimulation and implanted muscle substitutes are opening fantasy doorways for the orthopedically impaired ("New Research to Restore Body Functions," 1974, p. 82). "Functional neuromuscular stimulation or the activation of paralyzed muscles" is relevant to both restoration of function in paraplegics and improvement of control in persons with cerebral palsy (Hambrecht, 1975, p. 10). Researchers have been able to produce finger and wrist movements in quadriplegics by implanting electrodes into muscles that have nerves *from* the spinal cord, while lacking nerve paths from the brain *to* the spinal cord. Some problems remain to be solved before this laboratory finding can be translated into practical application, but this technique may, in the not-too-distant future, enable quadriplegics to use their hands to perform basic functions.

Have you ever watched a television program about a "bionic" person? In 1976 two very popular television programs were "The Bionic Woman" and "The Six Million Dollar Man." Both of these TV characters were supposed to have had serious accidents in which selected body parts were destroyed and then replaced in surgery by electronically operated, undetectable prostheses. "Pure science fiction," I snapped at my daughter when she alluded to the relationship between these TV characterizations and the real world of the physically disabled. A few weeks later I went on a tour of New York University Medical Center, Institute for Rehabilitative Medicine, and there, in a glass display case, was a model of an electronically operated lower arm and hand covered with a skinlike sheath. A myoelectric arm, activated by tiny electric impulses from the person's existing muscles. Shades of the bionic woman! I owe my daughter an apology. The gulf between actuality and fantasy grows narrower.

In the meantime biomedical engineers are working on the application of technological advances to everyday needs. Electronic letter boards have been devised which provide a means of communication for cerebral-palsied individuals who cannot speak and who lack the finger dexterity to type. One version of such a board (the Auto-Com) prints messages on a typewriter, a television screen, or a tape (Wendt, Sprague, and Marquis, 1975). Another version has all the letters of the alphabet displayed on a screen, where a light moves from letter to letter. The individual performs a movement that stops the light at the desired letter, which is then printed out by an electric typewriter (Williams,

1975). Another computer-assisted communications system was developed by Bell Labs engineers working in their spare time. This system features a kind of shorthand to speed up communication. Two letter codes have been devised for commonly communicated statements. For example, a youngster with cerebral palsy might punch the letters IC on the letter board and the sentence "I am cold" would appear on a television screen. This shorthand simplifies the motor demands on the cerebral-palsied individual, and diminishes the impatience that often is felt by the nondisabled person to whom the communication is addressed. Within a short time engineers expect to be able to make such systems compact enough to be fitted onto a wheelchair ("Computer Helps Students 'Talk,'" 1976, p. 7).

Medical researchers and engineers still have many problems to solve, but the progress made in the 1960s and 1970s has made possible a new freedom, a new quality of life for the physically handicapped. What technology has made possible, the society of man must now make a reality. While many of the technological developments of the 1970s are still being perfected, others are ready to be used. What we need is a better network of information and a reliable source of funding, so that all physically disabled persons can obtain the best of what is now available. Too many people are lying helpless in homes or hospitals because there isn't enough money for them, or because they just don't know how to obtain the benefits of modern medical technology. When the fruits of the research of the 1960s and 1970s have been perfected, will society be ready to provide all physically disabled persons with these life enrichers? Or will tens of thousands continue to be helpless because we are not prepared, while a lucky few are paraded about to display our technological genius?

NEW VISION FOR THE BLIND?

The *New York Times* article read: "The long-sought development of practical reading machines for blind people appears close to fruition. . . ." ("Text Goes In, Speech Comes Out of Machine," 1976, p. IV 6). For thousands of years blind persons had been dependent upon others to read to them. Then came Braille, a written language of their own, and the blind could read independently. Braille opened up a whole new world of communication. The Library of Congress began a national network of regional libraries to serve blind people. Large numbers of books were produced in Braille and lent to the blind throughout the country. To meet the needs of those who could not read Braille, "talking books"—i.e., books on records—were also produced in large numbers. Still, there was a time lag between need and availability. Still, there was much written that blind individuals could not read.

The blind turned to technology, and technology responded. The Optacon was a reading machine that first came off the production line in 1971 (Howe Society of Greater New York, 1974, p. 34). It was designed to give blind people immediate, direct access to all print materials. To read with the Optacon a blind person moves a miniature camera along a line of print with one hand. Signals from the camera are converted into a pattern of vibrating reeds on a tactile screen, which the person "reads" with a finger of his other hand. But those who have been blind from birth or early childhood have never read letters before. What they have read are the patterns of raised dots which constitute Braille. They have to be taught to recognize letter shapes and to read these shapes in the context of words. Even persons who have been blinded in later life have to be trained to acquire a reasonable reading speed when the visual cues they formerly relied on to recognize letters are no longer available to them. Some blind people will never be able to read via the Optacon because the diabetes that caused their blindness also caused a loss of sensation in their fingertips.

The search has taken another direction—machines that turn print into speech. Information from a camera is fed to a minicomputer, which in turn sends commands to a speech-producing device. Computerized speech at a rate of up to 200 words per minute results. Such machines are not yet perfected, but are on the way.

Technology has gone to work for the partially sighted too. Closed-circuit television (CCTV) systems are being used to make ordinary print legible to persons who could only read enlarged print before, and even that with difficulty. Again a camera is the starting point. The print that the television camera sees is electronically modified so that the image shown to the visually impaired person on a television screen is larger, has more contrast, and has less glare than the original. Many legally blind persons can read with the aid of CCTV systems.

Persons who are legally blind are also reading today because of advances in optometry. Telescopic lenses have improved visual functioning in some persons to the point where there is a debate as to whether such persons should be allowed to drive automobiles, even though they had been declared legally blind (Edelson, 1975, p. 78).

The variety of new electronic devices designed to provide greater independence and more freedom of choice for the blind is impressive. There are Braille electronic calculators and talking electronic calculators. There is a paper money identifier, developed by NASA, which can fit neatly into a shirt pocket (American Foundation for the Blind Newsletter, 1975, p. 9). There are compressed speech machines that allow for listening speeds up to two and a half times greater than normal speech production, without change in voice pitch. There are techniques for translating sheet music into Braille in fifteen minutes with the help of a computer, and there are Braille computer terminals. Ultrasonic spectacles can provide blind persons with auditory cues that tell about the distance, position, and surface characteristics of objects within the immediate environment. Canes using laser light can warn blind travelers about objects in their path and identify the position of these objects.

Technology is providing the possibility of fuller, more active, more independent lives for people with disabilities. Science and medicine are pushing further, pushing for the knowledge that will allow us to undo disabilities, to give sight to the blind, to help generate new brain cells, to reverse mental retardation, to cure psychosis. Already many miracles have been wrought. These dreams of today will be the realities of our futures.

"It looked like the bright spark of an arc weld. Have you ever seen an arc weld in the black of night? It had a slight whitish-blue cast to it. Much brighter than I had any idea it could be."

The audience, all blind, listened intently as the speaker, a blinded Korean war veteran, described the light flashes evoked when neurosurgeons stimulated electrodes implanted in his brain.

Leland, 45, . . . volunteered for an experimental brain operation to help scientists at the University of Utah's institute for biomedical engineering develop what they hope one day will be an artificial system of vision . . . a miniature system that would be worn like a pair of spectacles. A glass eye containing a sub-miniature camera would be implanted in the eye socket and held by eye muscles.

The camera would transmit various levels of light to a tiny computer or processor attached to the spectacles' frame. The images would be converted to signals and the data sent to electrodes under the skull, where the brain would create the image.

The hope is to develop a device that would enable the wearer to see outlines of letters well enough to read. . . . What has been demonstrated so far is that even though eyesight is lost, the brain's potential for vision remains intact.[2]

In the meantime there is much work to be done. Too few are benefiting from the techniques and products available now. We must reach out to them with the lifelines that we already have.

[2]By Arthur J. Snider, *Chicago Daily News* Science Editor, "Artificial Sight for the Blind?" *New York Post*, August 5, 1974, p. 22. Courtesy of Field Newspaper Syndicate.

REFERENCES

American Foundation for the Blind Newsletter, 10, no. 4 (1975), 9.

"Computer Helps Students 'Talk,' " *Crusader* (United Cerebral Palsy Association, Inc.), Winter 1976, p. 7.

EDELSON, E., "Victims of Low Vision Are Often Neglected—Despite New Visual Aids," *New York Daily News*, November 28, 1975, p. 78.

GOFFMAN, E., *Stigma*. Englewood Cliffs, N.J.: Prentice-Hall, 1963.

HAMBRECHT, F. T., "Applications of Technology to the Neurologically Handicapped," in *Research Report*, Vol. 2, United Cerebral Palsy Research and Educational Foundation, 1975.

Howe Society of Greater New York, *What's New in Electronic Arts for the Visually and Auditorily Handicapped*. New York: City University of New York, Institute for Research and Development in Occupational Education, 1974.

"New Research to Restore Body Functions," *Accent On Living*, 19, no. 1 (1974), 82-83.

"Rancho Arm Operated by Tongue," *Accent On Living*, 18, no. 4 (1974), 44-47.

RUSK, H. A., *Rehabilitation Research and Training Center Progress Report, RSA 16°P°56801/2°14. New York: New York University Medical Center, 1975.*

SNIDER, A. J., "Artificial Sight for the Blind?" *New York Post*, August 5, 1974, p. 22.

"Text Goes In, Speech Comes Out of Machine," *New York Times*, January 18, 1976, p. IV6.

WENDT, E., M. J. SPRAGUE, and J. MARQUIS, "Communication Without Speech," *Teaching Exceptional Children*, 8, no. 1 (1975), 38-42,

"Wheelchair Follows Orders," *New York Times*, May 4, 1975, p. 31.

WILLIAMS, G., "Science Reaches for Miracles," *Family Health*, 7, no. 9 (1975), 26-29, 64-66.

TEN

And Now You

I guess the goal of this book has been consciousness raising. Consciousness raising is important as a prelude to behavioral change. If this book has succeeded at all in sensitizing you to persons with disabilities, their hopes and goals, let's examine whether it has also readied you to examine your own behavior in this context.

What do you do when you meet a blind person? Slink away? Take his arm and push him someplace? Or identify yourself and relate as you would to anyone else? The last one, I hope.

What do you do when a friend who is the mother of a retarded child visits? Do you act as if she had no child, taking care not to allude to him? Do you refrain from talking about your children in her presence? Don't! Ask your friend about her child. Talk about your children, and listen when she talks about hers. (Don't stop being her friend because you feel uncomfortable.)

What do you do (if you're a teacher) when your principal tells you that a handicapped child is going to be placed in your class? Do you tremble in fright? Do you get angry and say, "That child needs a specialist?" Or do you begin to expand yourself as a teacher?

If you see a person in a wheelchair helping himself with a difficult physical task, what do you do? Rush to take over? Stand frozen in anguish and indecision? Let him do for himself, unless he seems to be in trouble. Then ask; don't assume. If he needs help, he'll tell you.

If you are an employer or work in a personnel office, what are you doing to give persons with disabilities a chance?

If you are a college student who babysits to make money, have you considered offering your services to the parents of a disabled child?

If you are in any way involved in the planning of new physical facilities, have you planned with awareness of the disabled?

If you see a disabled person acting disagreeably, do you retreat to the stereotype of the disabled as bitter and cruel in reaction to their disability, or do you remember that most people act disagreeably at times, often with justification?

If you meet a disabled person who is compatible with you in many ways, do you brush away the discomforts and inconveniences and allow yourself to become his (her) friend?

CODA

*A Bicentennial Declaration of Human Rights for Handicapped Persons**

When in the Course of human events, it becomes necessary for a people to dissolve the bonds which have constrained them, and to assume among the powers of the earth the separate and equal station to which the Laws of Nature and of Nature's God entitle them, a decent respect to the opinions of humankind requires that they should declare the causes which impel them to the declaration.

We hold these truths to be self-evident, that all people are created equal, that they are endowed by their Creator with certain unalienable rights, that among these are Life, Liberty and the pursuit of Happiness.

*Charles M. Westie, *A Bicentennial Declaration of Human Rights for Handicapped Persons*. Central Michigan University, Office of Career Development for Handicapped Persons. Reprinted by permission.

We further declare that for the physically handicapped, the paramount right is to be a person made whole by exercising human potentialities, most notably:

THE RIGHT TO CITIZENSHIP

No person shall be denied this right by inaccessible buildings or polling places. For each person it shall be made possible to vote, and to enter freely and do business independently in public buildings such as the courts, social service and employment offices, city halls, and county buildings.

THE RIGHT TO EDUCATE ONESELF

No physically handicapped person shall be denied equal opportunity to utilize educational institutions, libraries, museums, or other means of pursuing knowledge by reason of architectural, traditional, or attitudinal barriers.

THE RIGHT TO AN OCCUPATION
OR PROFESSION

No person shall be denied the right to enter any occupation or profession solely for reasons of disability, provided he or she can perform the duties of the occupation creditably.

THE RIGHT TO MAINTAIN HEALTH
AND PHYSICAL WELLBEING

Medical facilities shall provide equal access to all persons regardless of physical or other disabilities; moreover, public facilities shall be made generally available, identifiable, and accessible to handicapped persons including food service, restrooms, and places to have a drink of water or to rest when tired.

THE RIGHT TO RECREATION

No persons shall be denied access by reason of physical handicap to auditoriums, theaters, sports facilities, public parks and monuments, woodlands, rivers, lakes or other recreational or entertainment facilities open to the general public.

THE RIGHT TO INDEPENDENT LIVING

Handicapped persons shall not be denied accommodations in houses, apartments, hotels, dormitories, or barracks open to other persons, and shall be free to live with other persons of their choice.

THE RIGHT TO SAFE AND INDEPENDENT TRAVEL

No citizen, government regulatory agency, or public carrier shall prevent handicapped persons from equal access to any mode of transportation. Public agencies shall do all in their power to facilitate the safe movement of physically handicapped persons.

THE RIGHT TO LOVE

No citizen, agency, or any legislative, executive, or judicial branch of government shall deny to handicapped persons the relationships of friendship, love, and marriage through any means not applicable to all other persons.

THE RIGHT TO WORSHIP

Handicapped persons shall be afforded the means to enter places of worship independently and the right to attend public worship services.

THE RIGHT TO LIVE AND DIE WITH DIGNITY

No person shall be denied the right to live with dignity and, when finding life no longer bearable, to die with dignity, within the legal requirements of the state in which he or she lives.

We therefore declare, on the occasion of the two-hundredth birthday of our beloved country, that physically handicapped people are and of a right ought to be free and independent, and that such persons have the power to live as independent and full human beings. We who subscribe to this declaration shall do all things in our power to secure these rights, and for the support of this declaration we mutually pledge to each other our lives, our fortunes, and our sacred honor.

Index